PERSPECTIVES IN AFRICAN THEOLOGY

Perspectives in African Theology

VOLUME TWO

Je'adayibe Dogara Gwamna

AFRICA CHRISTIAN TEXTBOOKS

2014

Perspectives in African Theology
© 2014 by Je'adayibe Dogara Gwamna

Africa Christian Textbooks (ACTS)

ACTS Bookshop, International HQ, TCNN,
PMB 2020, Bukuru, Plateau State, 930008, Nigeria
GSM: +234 (0) 803-589-5328; E-mail: acts.jos@gmail.com
Website: http://www.acts-ng.com

ISBN: 978-978-905-211-0 Print
ISBN: 978-978-905-234-9 ePub
ISBN: 978-978-905-235-6 Mobi

ACTS has 11 branches:

Abuja (Garki, International Market)	0703 771 2858
Ilorin (UMCA)	0803 208 4031
Jos (JETS)	0803 923 4762
Jos (TCNN)	0803 946 8691
Kagoro (ETS)	0802 798 4408
Lagos (Ikeja, Underbridge Bus Stop)	0803 218 0523
Lagos (WATS)	0802 367 0628
Ogbomoso (NBTS)	0803 536 8021
Saminaka (TSNN)	0813 125 1284
Uyo (Obio Imo St)	0802 784 3266
Kenya (NEGST)	acts.kenya@gmail.com

DEDICATION

This book is dedicated to all Christian Contextualists in Africa.

CONTENTS

FOREWORD

In *Perspectives in African Theology, Volume 2*, Professor Dogara Je'adayibe Gwamna gives a detailed description and insightful critique of contemporary Christian theology and practices. His description and critique is well documented and clearly articulated, with an understanding review of up-to-date literature. However, instead of just providing a critique, as most scholars tend to do, Prof. Gwamna goes one step further and offers practical strategies for Christian leaders to address the challenges that face the African church.

Professor Gwamna has written an engaging and practical book of relevant issues that face the church in Africa, including the need to contextualize the Gospel with the modern African worldview, the burgeoning Pentecostal and charismatic movement, and the need for Christians to be salt and light in the public sphere. His readers will rapidly identify with the issues that have been raised and benefit by the practical strategies that are offered for building the church. His insight and understanding of the modern African church will enrich readers as they seek to advance the kingdom in their own spheres of influence.

Katrina Korb.
February 2014.

PREFACE

Since the publication of *Perspectives in African Theology* in 2008, Biblical scholars have commended the chapters contained therein due to their very topical and contextual nature. This has spurred me to produce a second volume in what might eventually become a series in this area of scholarly engagement.

Thus, *Perspectives in African Theology, Volume Two* is a seven-chapter book containing articles originally published in various journals and books and some which were presented in conferences. Some chapters, which contain material on Pentecostalism in Nigeria, derive in part from my participation as a Senior Researcher in the Nigerian Pentecostal and Charismatic Research Centre. Some of these articles include:

- "A Contextual Consideration of the Church, Culture and the Gospel in Africa," *Ogbomoso Journal of Theology*, 2012.
- "Jesus' Metaphor of 'Salt and Light' for Socio-Religious Transformation in Nigeria," S.O. Abogunrin (ed.), *Biblical Studies and Social Transformation in Africa*, Biblical Studies Series, No. 9, Nigerian Association for Biblical Studies (NABIS), Ibadan, 2012;
- "Understanding Paul's Contextualization Methods for Mission Engagement in Africa," *Renewal*, West Africa Theological Journal, Vol. 1. No.1, 2013;
- "Pentecostal Phenomenon and Growth in Nigeria," A Paper Presented at the Pentecostal and Charismatic Research Conference, held in Jos, 2011;

- "Pentecostalism and the Challenge of Hermeneutics and Application in Nigeria," *African Journal of Pentecostal and Charismatic Studies*, Vol. 1. No.1, 2013;
- "Of Charlatans and Magicians: An Understanding of Acts 8:9-25 in the Light of Pentecostal Experience in Nigeria." A Paper Presented at the Theological Educators in Africa (TEA) Conference, TCNN, Bukuru-Jos, 2011,
- "Theological Education and Transformation in Nigeria," A Paper Presented at Jos ECWA Theological Seminary, Jos, 2012.

It is my hope that these chapters will enrich teachers and students in Seminaries and Universities in the area of teaching and research on some theological issues in Nigeria and Africa as a whole.

It is also my conviction that in order to foster richer insights and understanding, African students, teachers and pastors need to increase their efforts to document and publish our theological thoughts and writings. The contextual engagement of theological issues in Africa demands that we present the Biblical messages within African perspectives in order to relate more meaningfully to the African people. I hope this volume will meet this challenge.

Except where otherwise stated, all Biblical quotations are taken from the New International Version (NIV, 2011).

Dogara Je'adayibe Gwamna, *far*
Keffi, November 2013.

ACKNOWLEDGEMENTS

I wish to thank those who assisted me in one way or the other towards the publication of this volume. I wish to thank Ahmad Muhammad Auwal who typed my manuscript and assisted in the formatting of this work. I wish to thank Dr. Dauda Andrawus Gava who read the book at the draft stage and made his editorial comments.

I thank Dr. Katrina Korb who read this work and provided tremendous insights and comments towards the improvement of this work. I thank her for writing the foreword to this book. I thank also Dr. Dauda Andawurus Gava, who read the draft of this book and made corrections and comments.

For other numerous readers of my previous volume whom I cannot practically mention, I am very grateful for your unceasing encouragement and prayers. I pray that God will reward your show of love. May you remain blessed.

Prof. Dogara Je'adayibe Gwamna, *far*.
November, 2013.

CHAPTER 1

CONTEXTUAL CONSIDERATION OF THE CHURCH, CULTURE AND THE GOSPEL IN AFRICA

Introduction

The puzzle of the interplay of the church, culture and the Gospel in Africa has been a long and controversial one. This chapter looks at the contextual approach to the question. Can they really mix? Are they reconcilable? The chapter raises certain presuppositions that help to direct this discourse, namely;

i.   A contextual approach towards looking at the church, culture and the Gospel is Biblical and the key towards evolving the ever-contending issues in Africa.

ii. A contextual look at the church, culture and the Gospel is necessary, timely and relevant in Africa today.

iii. A contextual consideration of the church, culture and the Gospel is practical in its appropriation, and can help to enrich Christianity in Africa.

iv. The church was founded in a culturally defined contextual background that shaped its message and theology.

Africa is witnessing a major current today in world Christianity. It is witnessing a "southward shift in the centre of gravity of global Christianity" (Walls 118). Africa's place in world Christianity today cannot be easily dismissed. In the words of Lamin Sanneh, "Africa has become or is becoming a Christian continent" (Sanneh, 36). Sanneh states that, "the statistical weight has moved Africa firmly into the Christian orbit" (36). The challenge this poses for the church in Africa is how it is able to relate to the culture of the people in a continent, where culture is so pervasive, strong and determines the worldview of a people's sub-total life experiences. As Walls reminds us, "issues of culture are at the heart of Christian faith" (Walls, 67). A brief clarification of some key terms in this chapter will help our discussion.

i. Church: Fleming notes that, "the word which Jesus used and which has been translated 'church' meant originally a collection of people, a meeting, gathering or community" (Fleming, 65). Guthrie, on the other hand, links the church to Jesus' teaching about the kingdom of God and notes that the church is a partial manifestation of the kingdom (Guthrie, 704). *Ekklesia*, which is used in the Septuagint (LXX) was used for the congregation of Israel, just as the Hebrew *qahál* was used to refer to God's people conceived as a new community especially related to the Messiah. Beginning on the day of Pentecost, the church emerged with power following the outpouring of the Holy Spirit and grew to "the ends of the earth," by the close of the first century A.D.

Chester and Timmis have asserted that the church is at the heart of the Gospel life and mission, (Chester and Timmis 37) and quoted Stott thus:

> The church lies at the very centre of the external purposes of God. It is not an accident of history. On the contrary, the church is God's new community. For this purpose, conceived out in history, a past eternity, being worked out in history and to be perfected in a future eternity, is not just to save isolated individuals and so perpetuate our loneliness, but rather to build his church, that is, to call out of the world a people for his own glory (37-38).

Chester and Timmis maintain that, "the Bible shows that we are communal creatures made to be lovers of God and of others," (38) and "the Church grows in a new community and a new identity" (39).

One of the distinguishing marks of the early church was *koinonia*, fellowship or communion living. Acts 2:42 says; "They devoted themselves to the apostles' teaching and to the fellowship, to the breaking of bread and to prayer." *Koinonia*, which is the New Testament word for community, is also linked to fellowship and sharing, and participation in Christian community is central to Christian mission (41).

ii. Culture: Culture is defined in many ways. "Culture in its broadest sense is cultivated behaviour, that is the totality of a persons' learned, accumulated experience which is socially transmitted, or more briefly, behaviour through learning" (online). It is also defined as, "the sum total of the learned behaviour of a group of people that are generally considered to be the tradition of that people and are transmitted from generation to generation" (online). From the definitions above, we can state that culture is a human social construct providing people with a worldview by which they are guided and identified. It shapes a people's world, provides values, norms and a philosophy in life. Thus, all human cultures have one form of culture, or the other. Culture is also dynamic as no culture is static. Other features of culture identified by Ademowo are that culture is adoptive, integrated, learned, shared and symbolic (Ademowo, 14).

Scholarly works on African culture exist. The classic work of Achebe, *Things Fall Apart*, depicts typical African traditional societies and the religious cultural worldview, of the Igbo and the missionary encounter, which led to the disruption of African social systems and what Ayandele calls the collapse of "pagandom Jericho-wise" in Africa (Metuh, 134).

Similarly, Mbiti, in his *African Religions and Philosophy* asserts that Africans were "notoriously religious," and that religion permeates all aspects of the African life (Mbiti, 1-3). According to Mbiti, "African people do not know how to co-exist without religion" (1-3). Scholarly works, by John Mbiti, Bolaji Idowu, Emefie Ikenga Metuh, Yusufu Turaki and others, show Africa's knowledge of God. In the words of Sanneh, "no missionary tutoring was necessary to establish the idea of a personal God" (Sanneh, 36).

Nevertheless, Western anthropologists, colonialists, missionaries and explorers easily dismissed Africa's sense of religion and denied Africa's cultural values of morality, awareness of God and capability for philosophical thinking (Ehusani, 77-79). Some of modern Africa's scholarly writings, such as Bolaji Idowu, John Mbiti, E. Ikenga-Metuh, Yusufu

Turaki, Samuel Waje Kunhiyop and others, have proven this to be untrue of Africans as these portrayals were influenced by the Western cultural biases of ethnologists, sociologists and missionaries, whose reaction to African traditions and culture–were coloured by European superiority cultural biases.

iii. Gospel: By "Gospel" here, we are referring to the corpus of the *kerygma,* namely, the proclamation of early Christian apostles centred on the life and teachings of Jesus Christ. The *kerygma,* was the core of the New Testament message that led to the foundation of the church and its growth. Paul calls the Gospel, the "power of God unto salvation for those who believe" (Rom: 1:6)

Africa and the Gospel Witness

Africa is not new to the Gospel. John Pobee states that, "the church has existed a long time in Africa" (Pobee, 47). It also "has a varied history." Tracing the historical significance of Africa to the gospel tradition, Foster writes:

> The North African coast is the southern shore of the Mediterranean. This area is prominent in Roman history, and it is prominent in church history too because it was the home of the greatest of the Latin Fathers (111).

Foster provides specific examples further:

> The African continent is full of associations with the early church-Tertullian, Cyprian, Clement, Origen, Augustine and the rest, which all African Christians should know and claim. The churches of Egypt and Ethiopia contributed much especially Ethiopia, which

became a Christian-ruled country in 350, the oldest in the world (116-135).

Early church fathers influenced early Christianity in many ways, as its theological minds and writers, and helped to shape early Christian theology and canon. They also sat in councils and developed part of the early Christian creeds. Usry and Keener corroborate Foster, when they note that European scholar Theodor Mommsen "acknowledged that, through Africa Christianity became the religion of the world" (Usry and Keener, 33). For Usry and Keener, "North Africa was one of the Gospel's securest homes" (33), "and this African empire probably remained more solidly Christian than Europe did" (39). For Mbiti, "Christianity in Africa is so old that it can rightly be described as an indigenous, traditional and African religion" (Usry and Keeener, 39).

Oden in his, *How Africa Shaped the Christian Mind*, corroborates the foregoing too by stating that; "cut Africa out of the Bible and Christian memory and you have misplaced many pivotal scenes of salvation history" (Oden 14). He states further, "this is the sweet kernel of the grain that fed Christian intellectual history before Constantine" (14). Oden notes significantly that:

> The Christian leaders in Africa figured out how best to read the law and prophets meaningfully, to think philosophically, and to teach the ecumenical rule of triune faith cohesively, long before these patterns became normative elsewhere (14).

Umoren has provided a three-phased historical Christian encounter in Africa as follows:

i.   The apostolic age in which the church came to Africa and left its intellectual and "episcopal vitality" before Islam came in the 7th century A.D.;

ii. The end of the Middle Ages with the Portuguese exploration of Africa.

In fact, within the second phase of Christian presence in Africa, Portuguese missionaries established contact with African peoples in the Canary Islands, Ceuta in Morocco (1415), Cape Verde Island (1445), Benin (1472), along the coast of Guinea, Equatorial Africa (Kongo) Angola, Mozambique and Kenya.

iii. The 19th century re-awakening of missionary endeavours in Africa through the revivalist movements in Europe (61-62).

Thus, it can be asserted that the Christian growth that Africa is witnessing presently, as a "global shift to the south," is actually a return of Christianity to its historical antecedents where it was marked by its early growth and impact.

Why a contextual consideration?

As is familiar from African scholarly discourse, missionary engagement in Africa has been "faulted" due to missionaries' "inability" or "failure" to appreciate African cultural beliefs and practices that were viewed by them as "primitive," "heathen" and "uncivilized," lacking any morality or philosophical reasoning.

Iwe captured the scenario this way:

> The missionaries were convinced of the immense superiority of the western culture, which Africa, as a cultural 'tabula rasa', must wholly absorb if it

> was to be rescued from the claws of paganism, savagery, barbarism and superstition. Such was the mentality of the early missionaries in Africa who did not penetrate the mind and culture of Africans. This cultural arrogance and superiority complex were definitely responsible for the strife between our culture and westernized Christian institutions and values (79).

The observation raised by Iwe is buttressed further thus:

> Many missionaries considered African culture and religion to be primitive and pagan. Consequently, these missionaries tried to force African Christians to reject most of their cultural and religious beliefs and practices. When African Christians read the Bible, they did not interpret what they read as condemning all or most of their cultural and religious beliefs and practices. Indeed, some African Christians believed that there were some similarities between the practices recorded in the Old and New Testaments of the Bible and their own cultural and religious practices. Faced with continued missionary opposition to adapting Christianity to African culture, some Christian leaders decided to leave mission churches and form their own independent churches that incorporated aspects of African cultural practices that they felt were not inconsistent with Christianity (Exploring Africa online, 6).

As has been noted from the above quotation, the emergence of the African Independent Churches (AICs) was a "reaction" to such missionary's insistence or negative attitude to Africa's cultural beliefs and practices, and the need to "Africanize Christianity," or to "contextualize" Christianity in Africa among other factors. Similarly, African scholars today easily

find what Wambutda refers to as "Hebrewisms in Africa,"
where Old Testament beliefs and practices find parallels
in African culture (Wambutda, 33-41). Thus, the call for
contextualization is hinged on the premises that the gospel
or the church must understand and relate to Africans, within
their cultural and religious context. Contextualization is
becoming popular in third world countries particularly in
Africa, as a process that seeks to relate the Gospel message
by taking note of Africa's rich cultural heritage. Charles Taber
provides a definition of contextualization as follows:

> Contextualization is the effort to understand and take
> seriously the specific context of each human group and
> person on its own terms and in all its dimensions –
> cultural, religious, social, political, economic, and to
> discern what the Gospel says to people in that context
> (Parshall, 32).

Gilliland also states:

> Contextualization theology is the dynamic reflection
> carried out by the particular church upon its own life
> in light of the word of God and historic Christian
> truth. Guided by the Holy Spirit, the church continually
> challenges, incorporates, and transforms elements of a
> cultural milieu, bringing these under the lordship of
> Christ. As members of the body of Christ interpret the
> word, using their own thoughts and employing their
> own cultural gifts, they are better able to understand
> the gospel as incarnation (12-13).

Gilliland lists six reasons why contextualization is the
appropriate method and spirit for missions today and for the
future:

i.   Contextualization guards against the imperialism of theology;

ii.   Contextualization provides for training in the Holy Spirit;

iii. Contextualization cultivates a mission-conscious Church;

iv.   Contextualization fosters the growth and multiplication of churches;

v.   Contextualization promotes multi-dimensional Gospel needs;

vi.   Contextualization opens the way for incarnational witness (13-23).

Gilliland emphasizes that contextual incarnation means that the message will make sense for each place and people, and that contextual incarnation utilizes cultural elements that are consistent with the gospel (23-25).

Cole has also added his voice by stating that, "in the WCC's third mandate, *missio dei* was regarded as key basis for contextualization" (Cole, 13). Cole has indicated the Biblical basis of contextualization in the New Testament, as the gospel moved from a Hebrew to a Hellenistic context and writes that "the spread of the Church from Jewish to Hellenistic culture presents us with Biblical precedents for contextualization"(14). By contextualization, we mean a process in which the gospel is presented in a way that not only makes sense to the African mind and heart, but which also penetrates his entire life. It arises from the fact as Umoren observes:

> Gospel faith has not found a home in the rich African soil, and that most Africans live in two worlds: the real world of their traditional culture and religion as well

as the superficial but prodigious life of Sunday-Sunday Christians (63).

Some believe that Christianity in Africa is not as integrated into the different dimensions of human life as was the traditional religion. Often Africans enter a Westernized church, but resort to the meaningfulness of traditional faith at crises (key) points in life (Umoren, 63). Such crisis moments provide them with options to patronize traditional religious medicine men, diviners, soothsayers and so on. It is often asserted that Islam made more inroads in Africa, because it was more accommodating to African culture than Christianity did. Kenny corroborates this assertion:

> In Africa, Islam is said to have an advantage because of easier and more realistic moral demands. A man may have more than one wife; divorce is allowed and is easy. Revenge is allowed. There is considerable practical toleration of participation in traditional religious practices. As Islam takes root and begins to grow among a people on the other hand, alcohol is forbidden, even though the ban is not always enforced (127).

Kenney buttresses this point further by noting that:

> Islam is sometimes made out to be part of African identity, a rallying point against colonialism. Even the Arabic names and Arabic cultural appendages of Islam are presented as traditional and now native to Africa, whereas Christianity is depicted as Western and foreign. This African image has won some points for Islam in Africa, but it is counterbalanced by the image of Christianity as progressive (127).

It is to be noted, however, that while some see contextualization, as a viable methodology towards engaging the gospel in Africa's cultural worldview, some others speak of Africanization of Christianity in Africa as "inculturation," "indigenization," "enculturation" and "accommodation," among others. Mbiti speaks of "dialogue between African religion and Christianity" (Mbiti online) and opposes the term "indigenization of the Gospel in Africa." Mbiti states:

> Christianity, which results from the encounter of the gospel with any given local or regional community/ society, is always indigenous and, by definition, culture bound. The gospel, on the other hand, is "God-given," and does not change.

Mbiti asserts that "Christianity has Christianized Africa but Africa has not yet Africanized Christianity" (181). Because of the early Christian presence in Africa and its unprecedented impact on the early centuries of Christianity as noted earlier, Christianity cannot be said to be a new and "a foreign" religion. Rather, it still remains a fact that the gospel's presence preceded European contact with the gospel.

Introducing African Culture

Africans have a cultural matrix that defines them as a people. It provides them with beliefs, values and practices. It is a worldview, characterized by awareness of God, sense of morality, sense of communality, sanctity of life, sense of the sacred, harmony and peaceful co-existence. In his *Biblical Christianity in Modern Africa*, O'Donovan provides what he calls "basic differences between African and European cultural

values" (21). This is O'Donovan's profile of African cultural
values and European cultural values.

Table 1.1. Basic differences between African and European cultural values (Donovan 21)

S/No	African culture	Western culture
1.	Strong community values (groups' participation, group decision).	Strong individualistic values (individual's initiatives, individual decisions).
2.	Community identity.	Individual identity.
3.	Community life-style.	Private living style.
4.	Extended family emphasis.	Immediate family emphasis.
5.	Holistic approach to life.	Categorical approach to life.
6.	Importance on the event.	Importance of schedules & clock time.
7.	People – oriented priorities.	Task-and goal-oriented priorities.
8.	Real-life (situational) thinking.	Abstract and academic thinking.
9.	Preference for real-life learning.	Preference for academic learning.
10.	Spiritual worldview.	Scientific worldview.
11.	Emphasis on spoken communication.	Emphasis on written communication.

S/No	African culture	Western culture
12.	Emphasis on spoken agreements based on relationships between people.	Emphasis on written agreements based on policies created by committees.
13.	Respect for the elderly.	Respect for educated.
14.	Traditional inherited leadership.	Elected (democratic) leadership.
15.	Death is a passing into the spirit realities.	Death is practical problem (survivors need counseling & support).
16.	Resolve conflict through a mediator.	Resolve conflicts face to face.
17.	Practical (ritual) response to spirit realities.	Intellectual response to spirit realities.
18.	Practical (ritual) approach to religion.	Intellectual approach to religion.
19.	Vulnerability seen as weakness.	Vulnerability seen as strength.
20.	Much interest in the spirit world.	Little interest in the spirit world

From O'Donovan's differentiation of African and European cultural values, African values are more religiously derived, and closer to the Gospel values that make it easier and more practical for appropriation and application than the Western Europeanized values.

However, African traditional beliefs and practices have suffered many setbacks, as "they have been misinterpreted and misunderstood." According to Anne Nabimiyu–Wasike, "Christian churches devalued traditional African religion by linking it to paganism or heathenism," (47) and "the problem is how to set the African mind and heart free from the colonial influence that committed injustices against the African people while Christian churches looked on" (Wasike, 47).

There is the need, therefore, to correct "past errors" as she articulates:

> Christian churches in Africa have to come up with theologies that will seriously criticize the African past experience that has led to the present condition in order to come up with clear, prophetic and visionary statements that will give guidance to the African people for the future (47).

One of the distinguishing marks of African culture is the use of names. In my *Gbagyi Names: Religious and Philosophical Connotations*, I argued that Gbagyi names convey meanings and are dictated by circumstances of birth and other social contexts (Gwamna, 26). Names provide identity and define one's destiny. Ehusani puts it this way:

> The African name is an important vehicle of cultural identity. By virtue of their rich religious, anthropological and social content, African names. . .
> are part and parcel of those elements in African culture that go to make African personhood unique (Ehusani, 124).

Thus, the importance of names among Africans cannot be over-emphasized. Metuh corroborates this in the following terms:

> Names are not just identification marks put on people. Every Igbo name has a meaning, and people are not given names in haste, for the name is supposed to represent the most cherished thought in the mind of the giver at the time the name is given (Metuh, 44).

As a result of nationalists' consciousness and struggle, African nationalists spearheaded a change from western and Christian names to African ones in order to retain African identity. However, Biblical names also convey significant meanings. For example, New Testament passages discuss the significance of names. In Mark 9:39 Jesus said, "no one who does a miracle in my name can in the next moment say anything bad about me." In Mark 16:17, Jesus said, "and these signs will accompany those who believe. In my name they will drive out demons, they will speak in new tongues." Peter healed the lame man by the Beautiful Gate in Jerusalem "in the name of Jesus" (Acts, 3:6), and exploits of the Apostles were wrought through the power of the name of Jesus. It is also in the name of Jesus that salvation can be received (Acts, 4:12). Paul writes, "God has exalted him to the highest place and gave him the name that is above every name, that at the name of Jesus every knee should bow, in heaven and on earth and under the earth, and every tongue confess that Jesus Christ is Lord" (Phil. 2: 9 – 12). From the foregoing, therefore, it shows that the name of Jesus conveys power, healing and salvation. Thus, the African belief about names can be appropriated with the

Biblical witness, in order to enrich it as the Gospel interacts within the African milieu.

Part of African tradition and culture stems from the Africans and their belief in witchcraft and sorcery. Kunhiyop writes that, "almost all African societies believe in witchcraft in one form or another. It is the traditional way of explaining the ultimate cause of any evil, misfortune or death" (377). For Kunhiyop, "in the African mind, witchcraft is real and is considered the enemy of life" (378). The Gbagyi in Central Nigeria perceived witchcraft as the major source of evil and, therefore abhorred its belief and practice.

When the missionaries and Europeans came to Africa, they dismissed Africa's belief in witchcraft as superstitious and failed to understand the African worldview, in relation to witchcraft belief and practice. The resurgence of witchcraft beliefs and practices in Africa today, is a major challenge to Christianity that calls the Gospel to be able to answer and address witchcraft issues.

Kombo corroborates this challenge to Christianity when he writes that:

> Christianity should make better use of its claim to have the power to liberate people from the world of evil spirits: a world that is similar to the world of witchcraft. Exorcisms, or casting out of evil spirits, a decidedly biblical practice, could be useful in helping persons who operate in the realm of witchcraft to break free of this insidious belief and practice (Kombo 84).

Of course, some elements of Africa's cultural beliefs and practices attracted negative condemnation by missionaries as they were considered inconsistent with the Gospel, including polygamy, twin killings, ritual killings, shrines, altars and "idolatry," masquerades, chieftaincy title-taking and their rituals, nudity and "sexual pervasion," *osu* caste system, among others. The *osu* caste system's beliefs and practices among the Igbo have come under severe criticism today, as its belief and ritual practices have continued till date. Chidili, has defined *osu* as "symbolic human immolation or ritual slavery...once one becomes *osu* he is no more regarded as a human being" (223).

Chidili identifies *osu* with *alusi*, "a house name in Igboland...a human fabrication imbued with spirit, purposely designed for protection, for defense, or to avenge, or to mete out an outright killing of one's adversaries" (224). Chidili also links *alusi* to the *Okija* shrine, which involves human sacrifice, as its votaries patronize it in their quest for power, wealth and fame (230). *Okija* shrine is still patronized by politicians and top government job seekers for power, position and influence in some parts of Igboland, as well as among some Nigerians including some "nominal Christians" (*Newswatch*, 14-20).

The Church and Culture in Africa

The ever-compelling question for the church in Africa is how to relate with culture. This reality is pertinent and is a major challenge for the church. The church has been suspicious and critical of culture, because of its tendency to influence and possibly "corrupt" the Gospel. The church perceives that an unguarded romance with culture is capable of leading to syncretism. According to Kraemer, syncretism is "a systematic attempt to combine, blend and reconcile inharmonious, even often conflicting, elements in a so-called synthesis" (Kraemer, 392).

In Africa today, what we are witnessing with the Gospel is what could be referred to as the "hybridization of the Gospel," with the diffusion of culture, because of the contextualization of western values, and African traditional practices. The church needs to safeguard some of these tendencies in Africa, in order to maintain the integrity of the Gospel. Some of these tendencies are addressed below:

i. The church needs to articulate theological issues in a way that will engage with Africa's cultural elements, including those that are consistent with the Bible as well as those that are not.

ii. The church needs to discourage negative cultural practices that continue despite the Gospel presence in Africa. The church must confront the *osu* caste system among the Igbo in eastern Nigeria, in order to deliver them from the "bondage" dehumanization and slavery status that the *osu* are reduced to. Similar ritual shrines like the *alusi* in Igboland and the *Okija* ritual shrines in South-East, Nigeria, which promote human ritual killings, have continued to attract "nominal Christians" for patronage (Tell, 12-20).

The church in Africa needs to engage African cultures with the aim of constructively correcting their worldview with the Gospel message. Flemming provides such a model in his discussion of Paul at Athens. For Flemming, "Paul's strategy in Acts 17 involves both constructive and corrective engagement of his hearers' beliefs and worldviews" (199). Flemming states further:

> Paul's ministry in Athens in Acts 17 offers contemporary Christians an example of a magnificent balance, between an "identification" approach that proclaims the gospel in culturally relevant forms on the one hand, and a "transformational" approach that resists compromising the gospel's integrity, in a pluralistic culture on the other. Whether called to become "as a Jew to the Jews" within a familiar culture, or "as a Greek to the Greeks," among culture different from our own, it is the church's constant challenge to herald the good news – under the guidance of the Spirit – with that same passion for both contextual relevance and courageous fidelity to the transforming word of salvation (208).

It is to be noted also that in Paul's model of cultural sensitivity and creativity in proclaiming the Gospel, he did not syncretize his message or compromise its theological integrity. Michael has supported Fleming, by recognizing the need for the church in Africa to dialogue and engage African culture towards the goal of transforming it, in the light of Biblical revelation (Michael, 19).

iii. As a result of urbanization, migration, population explosion, globalization, and other factors today in Africa, African culture has come under severe cultural conflict and continuous interaction. The challenge for the Church is to be able to present the Gospel, in a way that will break the intercultural barriers consistent with the Gospel as it penetrates Africa. The early church witnessed intercultural growth in Africa, because of its ability to penetrate people's traditions and cultures.

iv. The need for the church to rediscover Africa's traditional religious spirituality has also been stressed. The church needs to contextualize the early church experience of communal love, fellowship and sharing, with Africa's communal living. The typical individualistic tendencies, which have influenced Africa through Western secularized worldviews and values, need to be discarded. Awoniyi has noted some "indigenous spirituality in Nigeria," which needs to be "appropriated," to include Africa's worship, emphasis on divine healing and divine health, and emphasis on prayer, among others (122-143). The ability of the church to incorporate elements of traditional African culture and the Gospel has been noted among the Charismatics and Pentecostals, in Africa whose tremendous growth today is partly attributed to their contextualized efforts (Awoyini, 130).

v. It has also been noted that language (vernacular) plays a vital role, as a vehicle of contextualization of the Gospel that the church in Africa needs to take seriously.

Sanneh has stressed this well in his writings. In fact, Sanneh shows how the vernacular power in the translation of the *confessio fidei*, of the pygmies of the Congo, left a very lasting impact among them (52). Sanneh also shows how the translation of the name of God in Yoruba and the Maasai of East Africa created great impact (60). He concludes that "such evidence is assurance too, that the indigenizing and inculturation of the Gospel stand to benefit the wider church" (60).

Mbiti also supports this position by showing how African Christological titles are emerging in Africa in its "dialogue, between Christianity and African religion" (2). Mbiti states, "African Christianity has put Jesus at both the centre and the peripherals. It has embraced classical and traditional Christology, but has added its own understanding of who Jesus Christ is" (4).

Mbiti says:

> These contextual titles are strongly coloured by African traditional religion. So, Africans embrace a Christian faith because of Jesus Christ, who is a new element which has captured their attention (4).

Mbiti provides examples of such Christological titles in Africa, such as Jesus the "Advisor," "Big tree," "Bulldozer," "Friend," "Liberator," "Master physician," "Expeller of Evil," the "big boat," etc. This is reflected even in songs composed and sung by African Christians. Mbiti concludes that, "Christology becomes the most intensely creative encounter between Christianity and African songs" (5).

Laing also recognizes the need for a synthesis of the Gospel and culture, and states "Christianity, for it to be true to itself, must allow itself to be translated into the culture of its new recipients on their own terms" (167). Laing notes that Christianity is a vernacular faith (166).

Thus, this approach and the call for dialogue is encapsulated in Adamo's "African Cultural Hermeneutics," defined as "the Biblical interpretation that makes African social cultural context a subject of interpretation" (2).

Conclusion

The imperative of the interplay of the church, culture and the Gospel in Africa cannot be taken for granted. It is necessary in order to avoid the "flaws" of past Christian encounter. Africa's rich cultural heritage provides immense resources, for the Gospel to be enriched by it.

The cultural challenge to the Gospel in Africa is still pervasive, with the resurgence of Africa's cultural practices, which seems to pose new challenges to African Christianity. Dialogue of culture and the Gospel is not a call towards syncretism, but the attempt to adapt positive essential elements of African culture, that are consistent with the Biblical witness. The church has a role in moderating the type of Christianity that, eventually, emerges in Africa in order to avoid hybridization of the Gospel that compromises its universal essence and application. The church in Africa must engage in theological discourse on contemporary issues that affect Christians in Africa in order to return to the legacies of the early church years (in Africa). It is, then, that Africa will play its prophetic role in this divine mandate that must be fulfilled in this age.

CHAPTER 2

JESUS' METAPHOR OF 'SALT AND LIGHT' FOR SOCIO-RELIGIOUS TRANSFORMATION IN NIGERIA

Introduction

Biblical studies, theological discourse and engagement in Africa are witnessing a shift from the theoretical, to the more practical existential realities of the people. This is also part of the contextualization efforts by African scholars in which such perspectives and methodologies have emerged focusing on issues that relate to people's daily experiences. Such theologies include political theology, theology of reconstruction, social theology, grassroots theology and ministry of social transformation, among others (Pierli, 24). Africa today, is in need of socio-religious transformation that will see Africa develop from a continent of under-development and inter-dependence to a more sustainable one. As this vision of transformation in Africa continues, biblical and theological engagement, interpretation and application, are being challenged to provide practical and meaningful responses in this direction.

Biblical studies is richly endowed with answers towards such responses. Biblical history and its prophetic tradition are replete with similar experiences that were addressed at various times. The scandal we have in Nigeria today of the enormous disparity between the rich and the poor, with the attendant consequences of social marginalization and economic exploitation, is treated extensively in both the Old and New Testaments.

The *Christian Rural and Urban Development Association of Nigeria* (CRUDAN) noted this challenge:

> While the church in Nigeria has been experiencing rapid growth numerically over the past years, there has also been an increase in injustice, oppression, corruption, mismanagement of resources, nepotism, ethnic conflicts and political instability within Nigeria and most other African countries (CRUDAN, 2).

This scenario, has led to high levels of poverty affecting an increasing number of people. CRUDAN further notes, "our challenge is to release the Bible to speak to all phases of human transformation. The Bible must be the bedrock and ultimate authority for any social change sought by Christians" (6). McCain (a) corroborates this when he notes that, "in fact the Bible is a progressive unfolding of God's strategy for restoring the world back to what God originally created it to be. It is a book of transformation, or more simply, a book of change" (1).

The Human Development Index (HDI) of 2013, ranked Nigeria at 153 out of 186 countries that were ranked (Nigeria: New Humand Devt. Report online, 1). Life expectancy in Nigeria is placed at 52 years old while other health indicators reveal that only 1.9 percent of the nation's budget is expended on health (1). The population dynamics display profound inequities and distortions, with one of the highest inequality levels in the world (1). The poverty level is so high despite Nigeria being a rich country with vast resources. Nigeria manifests high differential access to basic infrastructure, education, training and job opportunities. Unemployment and underemployment have continued, giving rise to crime and other social vices.

Musa expresses this point clearly:

> Indeed, the scale of poverty is widespread in Nigeria. One only needs to visit the urban slums and the rural areas to get a feel of the magnitude of suffering most Nigerians are going through. People are living in substandard houses, dirty and unhygienic environments; unable to eat balanced nutritious food; unable to send their children to good schools; lacking access to portable water, lacking good roads, having no access to health facilities, et cetera. The trend implies that poverty is on the increase (21).

It is in this context that this discourse on Jesus' Sermon on the Mount, particularly as it relates to his pronouncement that Christians are the "salt and light of the world," is situated and understood.

The Sermon on the Mount

The Sermon on the Mount (Matt.5-7) constitutes Matthew's particular narrative of Jesus' teaching. In Luke, it is called the sermon on the plain (Lk. 6:17). Doriani observes that, "among Jesus' teachings, the Sermon on the Mount is perhaps the most beloved, the least understood, and the hardest to obey" (1). The Sermon on the Mount, which was addressed to Jesus' disciples, is considered to contain the loftiest standards for human conduct ever conceived. It contains values for society living. It is penetrating and strenuous in its commands. Its challenging ethic is relevant and calls for application today.

The Sermon on the Mount has been considered in many ways over the years. For example, Thomas Aquinas, a medieval theologian and philosopher, suggested that ordinary Christians do not need to observe the sermon's hardest laws. He thought that the Bible presents a two-tiered ethic: the first tier applies to every Christian, the second tier (the counsel of perfection) is expedient, not mandatory (4). For Augustine, in the Sermon on the Mount, any serious reader will find "the perfect pattern of the Christian life" (Mounce, 340). Some call it a "charter for world peace" (Mounce 340). For Wilson, "the Sermon on the Mount is the constitution of the kingdom" (50). Ghandi, declared it the world's finest collection of ethical teaching (Mounce, 340). Jeremias sees the Sermon on the Mount as a catechism, designed for Jewish Christians, while for Luke it was designed for Gentile Christians.

On the other hand, Davies regards the sermon as the "Christian answer to Jamnia," a kind of Christian Mishnaic counterpart to the formulation that took place there. The reconstruction at Jamnia was not only Judaism's conscious confrontation with Christianity in a giant assertion to survive, but also the outside stimulus for the evangelist to formulate the way of the New Israel (Mounce, 340).

The contents of the sermon have led some to refer to it as a new *Christian manifesto*, an *interim ethic* that is nearly impossible to obey. The Sermon on the Mount contains sections on *thesis* and *antithesis* of Jesus' commands, the

Beatitudes (blessed passages) and thematic references to prayers, fasting, giving and so on.

Mounce has provided three models, or approaches to the study and understanding of the Sermon on the Mount including:

i. The Literalist View: This view takes the Sermon on the Mount literally and is applied consistently. For example, Leo Tolstoy, the Russian novelist and social reformer, taught that if mankind would literally obey the demands of the Sermon on the Mount, the existing evils of society would vanish and history would usher in a utopian kingdom (340). Tolstoy's proposition was because the Sermon on the Mount contains the moral principles required for any serious societal transformation. Doriani has indicated that some early Protestants favoured a simple literal reading of the sermon, and saw Jesus as the supreme teacher who presented laws that we should strive to obey, whatever the cost (5).

ii. Qualification View: This view denies that the ethical demands of Jesus are unattainable. It insists that Jesus was teaching general principles rather than issuing specific orders.

iii. Limited View: This view limits the demands of the law. For example, Roman Catholicism distinguishes between precepts (binding on all and essential for salvation) and counsels (for the select few and leading to salvation). This view is also tempered by

> pleading special circumstances as was held by Weiss
> and Schweitzer with their *interim ethic* thesis.

From these views therefore, it becomes clear that there is the
need for a balance in describing the kingdom, its values and
its challenges. It is with this background that we now turn to
the main text of our discussion, namely Matthew 5:13:16. It
reads:

> You are the salt of the earth. But if the salt loses its
> saltiness, how can it be made salty again? It is no
> longer good for anything except to be thrown out and
> trampled by men. You are the light of the world. A city
> on a hill cannot be hidden. Neither do people light a
> lamp and put it under a bowl. Instead they put it on
> its stand and it gives light to everyone in the house.
> In the same way, let your light shine before men, that
> they may see your good deeds and praise your Father
> in heaven (NIV).

The second corpus of the Sermon on the Mount after the
Beatitudes was Jesus' pronouncement to the disciples in vv.
13-16. Jesus told the disciples that: "you are the salt of the
earth." Common salt, or sodium chloride, is an abundant
substance in nature. Found worldwide, it is a common item in
every house and is used for a multiple of purposes. No wonder,
Pliny says, "without salt, human life cannot be sustained"
(Matthew Henry's Commentary, 44). Salt was obtained from
the marshes along the seashore in Cyprus and from the salt
lakes in the Dead Sea in Israel (Zeph. 2:9). The use of "salt and
light" metaphors are paralleled in Mark 9:50 and Luke 14:34,
which some scholars speculate as originating from the "Q"
document. However, while Matthew 5:13 emphasizes that the

disciples must be a blessing and a preservative in the world,
Mark 9:50 emphasizes that they must be faithful to their
covenant relationship with one another. Luke emphasizes that
they must maintain allegiance to Christ.

Biblical background of the use of salt

Salt is mentioned in the Bible more than 32 times. In the Old
and New Testaments, salt played diverse roles and functions
as follows:

i.   Salt provided taste and added flavour. It was a
     seasoner (Job. 6:6).

ii. It was used to season fodder for cattle (Is. 30:24).

iii. Salt was used as an antiseptic and medicine. Ezekiel
     16:4 provides a hint of Jewish practice of rubbing
     newborn babies with salt, as well as cutting the
     umbilical cord and washing with water. The priests
     were to sprinkle salt on the bull and sacrifice them
     as burnt offering to the Lord. Similarly, Elisha healed
     the poisonous spring near Jericho by throwing salt
     into it (2 Kings 2:19).

iv. Salt was also used as part of sacrificial meals (Lev.
     2:13). Thus "the food of God," was salted (Lev. 21:22,
     Ezek. 43:24).

v.   Salt was used to ratify covenants (Num. 18:19, 1
     Chron. 15:28, Lev. 2:13, 2 Chron. 13:5). "Covenant
     salt" became a symbol of perpetual obligation.
     For example, David received the promise of an
     everlasting kingdom from Yahweh by a "covenant

of salt" (2 Chron. 13:5). Covenants were generally confirmed by sacrificial meals and salt was always present (Ezek. 43:24). Today, when the Arabs say, "there is salt between us," or "he has eaten of my salt," it means partaking of hospitality, which cemented friendship (Polland, 3). "Eating the salt of a man meant deriving one's substance from him."

In fact, once an Arab had received in his tent even the worst of his enemies and had eaten salt (food) with him, he was bound to protect his guest as long as he remained.

vi.   Salt was also used as part of daily pay (Ezra, 6:9). According to the Roman writer, Pliny, Roman soldiers were to be paid in salt. The Latin word *salarium* translated "salary" today possibly originated from here (Nickerson, 1). The importance of salt in commerce is also known during the medieval period, while in Nepal and the Sahara salt was used in trade (Salt in the Bible online, 5). Salt was a valuable commodity that was highly regarded. Salt pits were a source of revenue to the rulers in the country (Josh. 15:62; Zeph. 2:9). There is an indication that at Taricheae on the Sea of Galilee, salting of fish, a staple article of commerce was extensively carried out (Nickerson, 2).

vii. Salt was also one of the spices that were traditionally used to prepare a body for burial in Biblical times (Hirsch, 2). The Old Testament mentions the "valley of salt" where two memorable victories of Israelite army took place.

> (a) That of David over the Edomites (2 Sam 8:1b, 1 Chron. 18:12), and
>
> (b) That of Amaziah (2 Kings 14:7, 2 Chron. 25:11ff).

viii. Salt is also mentioned along with other fragrant spices for anointing (Ex. 30:34-35).

ix. Luke 14:35a mentions it for manure. Inferior salt was added to manure.

x. Paul used it to refer to wisdom in speech. He said, "let your speech be always with grace, seasoned with salt, to answer every man" (Col. 2:4).

Salt was used metaphorically to refer to Israel (Hirsch 2) and Gundry notes that salt lent itself to metaphorical use (2). Old Testament prophets stood as moral watchdogs of Israelite society, as they salted the Israelite nation.

Hirsch and others have noted that, "owing to the fact that salt is referred to in the Bible as symbolizing the covenant between God and Israel, its importance is particularly pointed out by the Rabbis" (3). A "covenant of salt" (Num. 18:19) was interpreted to mean that salt was used by God on the occasion, in question, to signify that it should never be lacking from sacrifices. For the Rabbis, just as sacrifices could not be offered without priests, so they could not be offered without salt. After the destruction of the Temple, the table set for meals was considered an altar and the Rabbis recommended that salt be put upon it, and that blessing should not be recited without salt (Hirsch, 3).

In fact, the Rabbis likened the Torah to salt, for, as the world could not do without salt, neither could it do without the Torah. Salt was recommended for draining the blood from meat, and vegetables were salted in the field to make them fit for the tithe. Salt was a remedy for toothache, women were accustomed to hold a grain of salt on the tongue in order to prevent unpleasant odours in the mouth, and Rabbis recommended that a small amount of salt be eaten at the conclusion of every meal (Hirsch 3). In Rabbinic literature, also, salt was a metaphor for wisdom and intelligence, which was re-echoed by Paul in Colossians 4:6 (Ferguson, 63).

From the foregoing, the symbolism of salt includes among others: hospitality and antiseptic, durability, fidelity and purity. It also symbolized incorruptibility, wisdom and permanence. Jesus knew all these derivative meanings when he applied the same to the disciples. In other words, Jesus was saying that his disciples and followers are the positive aspects of salt and they are meant to salt the world in which they have been called, to effect positive transformation. However, when they fail to effect any positive impact, they become "saltless", and "worthless" as was the *bituminous salt* which was only good to be trampled upon, near the temple to prevent sliding during winter.

Christians as the "light of the world"

The second metaphor that Jesus used in this passage is that Christians are the light of the world. Light was the first thing God created (Gen. 1:3). God is always associated with light (Ps. 27:1, cf 2 Sam. 22:29, Is. 10:17). Serving God is described as "walking in his light" (Is. 2:5) and a light to others (Is 42:6; 49:6, 60:3). God's Word is light (Ps. 119:105 cf v. 130, Prov.

6:23, Is 5:4). It is used also in the Old Testament as a symbol of goodness, uprightness and blessing (Ps. 97:11).

Jesus talks here in the passage of two sources of light:

i.   A light from a city set on a hill; and

ii.   A light from a lamp set on a lamp stand.

Ferguson has observed that, "city dwellers in the modern world rarely, if ever, experience total darkness" (63). By contrast, those listening to Jesus who lived in rural communities; knew the significance of a city set on a hill like Jerusalem. In addition, "in Jesus' day, there was a city called Safed in the northwest of Galilee. It was a city set on a hill, and could have been in view while Jesus was teaching" (Morris, 316).

Jesus, therefore, gave it a dramatic twist, when he said he, not Jerusalem, was the light of the world and his disciples were to share in that mission. When one is in darkness one cannot see clearly. One loses direction and bearing. It blurs vision. Jesus had said in Matthew 6:23, "if then the light within you is darkness, how great is that darkness" (cf. 2 Pet. 1:19). Lampstands provided lighting in homes in Palestinian society and were popular among housewives. Light could not function in its true essence when it was hidden under a bushel.

Jesus had taught his disciples that he is the light of the world (Jn. 8:12). John used the imagery of light, in relation to Jesus in other places. For example, John 1:4 "in him was life, and the life was the light of men." "The light shines in the darkness, and the darkness has not overcome it." Leon Morris notes that, "the coming of Jesus meant the coming of the divine light to bring mankind illumination and salvation"

(316). Contact with light influences conduct. It is the Gospel of Jesus which brings light to the Gentiles: "to open their eyes that they may turn from darkness to light and from the power of Satan to God" (Acts 26:18 cf. Eph. 5:14). God has also called Christians "out of darkness into his marvelous light" (1 Pet. 2:9). Thus, Jesus saw light as a useful way to characterize the whole life of the Christian (Latourette, 503).

We live, today, in a world which has lost its moral bearings, and is blind to the consequences of such. Jesus says, Christians are the light bearers. They are meant to shine openly, willingly and with a purpose. They are to become beacons. They are to be spectacles to the world, due to their good works. Hence, Christians are the candlesticks, the "lamp stands," who must shine to the world just as John the Baptist in his day (Jn. 5:35). As lamps, they are to shine and cannot be hidden. It is foolhardy, therefore, when lamps that are meant to give light are hidden under bushels. It is like salt losing its saltiness. They must perform the function in which they are meant to be. It is a call and a command to be good for something.

Christians and the challenges of socio-religious transformation in Nigeria

What then is the significance of Jesus' saying to Christians in Nigeria for socio-religious transformation? Answering this question requires referring to Latourette, who rightly noted that:

> No life ever lived on this planet has been so influential
> in the affairs of men as that of Christ...From that brief
> life and its apparent frustration has flowed a more

> powerful force for the triumphal waging of man's long
> battle than any other ever known by the human race
> (503).

In other words, Latourette has identified the impact Jesus made as the most lasting in human history. For Latourette, the transforming force of Jesus remains unprecedented in human history (503). The penetrating influence of Jesus to transform lives, cultures and nations is still a continuing human experience, in this 21st century world of digital technology and information that has transformed our world. Stott captures this major challenge:

> There can surely be no doubt that our Lord Jesus Christ
> wants his values and standards to prevail. For he loves
> righteousness and hates evil (Psalm 45:7) wherever
> they are found. So he sends his people out into the
> world both to preach the gospel and make disciples,
> and to sweeten the whole community and make it more
> pleasing to God, more just, more participatory, more
> free (137).

Applying Jesus' values and standards, in order to sweeten and lighten the world and the human community, requires that Christians become the true salt and light of the world. Reflecting on this, further, Stott identifies what he calls, "the truths of salt and light," which are relevant to our application here thus:

i.   Christians must be radically different from non-Christians. Jesus intended that Christians be as different as light from darkness and salt from decay. Christians do not have to compromise with the world today under a false maxim that, "if you cannot beat them, you join them." In fact, the reverse of this dictum should guide Christian behavior in Nigeria, namely, "if you cannot beat them, you quit." That is a challenge and a call to Christian holy living, to being radically different (see Rom. 12: 2).

ii.   Christians must permeate non-Christian society, Christians are called to live and influence the world. Jesus said, "They are not of the world, even as I am not of it" (Jn. 17: 16). Jesus has called us to penetrate and permeate the world with values, standards and lifestyles that will sweeten the world giving it light, not being swallowed up or consumed by society, through its permeating influences. Christians can prevent this through their words and deeds. Nigeria can be radically transformed today, if Christians live to their calling and become worthy of their salt.

iii. Christians can influence and change non-Christian society. Salt and light are both effective commodities. They change the environment into which they are introduced (145). Stott puts it graphically:

> It may be argued that salt and light have complementary effects. The effect of salt is negative; it hinders bacterial decay. The influence of light is positive; it illuminates the darkness. Just so, the influence of Christians on society is intended by Jesus to be both negative and positive (promoting the spread of truth and goodness and especially of the gospel) (145).

Stott however blames "our habits as Christians for our failure to check deteriorating trends" around us, of societal injustice, racial conflict, violence in the streets, corruption in high places, sexual promiscuity and scourge of HIV/AIDS (Sider, 163).

When the church promotes injustice, ethnicity, favouritism and corruption, it becomes incapable of influencing any transformation as it lacks the moral force to effect any change. When the church is incapable of changing these evil tendencies in our society, it has literally lost all its value. It has lost its taste. It becomes a lamp that is "hidden under the bushel," which Jesus had cautioned against. That dilemma confronts the church in Nigeria today. The church needs to wake up from its slumber and provide the guiding light, and be the salt that it is meant to be, rather than to join as vanguards and comrades in perpetrating evil and other forms of societal decay, that we have found in Nigeria.

How can Christians be salt and light to the world? Christians can be salt and light today, by their engagement in social actions and responsibilities that are practical steps and strategies towards impacting the world. Ronald J. Sider has defined social action as, "that set of activities whose primary goal is improving the physical, social, economic, and political well-being of people through relief, development, and structural change" (Sider, 163). The primary intention of social action is preventing starvation, empowering the poor and improving social structures, so that persons created in God's image can enjoy more of the wholeness the Creator intended, during their three score years and ten (Stott,

145). Stott sees Christian responsibilities as hinged on social responsibilities that are also the fruit of evangelism (145).

Missionaries arriving in Nigeria came with the Gospel and social action. The establishment of schools, hospitals and other infrastructural developments was a major transformation force and tool in the socio-religious lives of the people. In fact, it was one of the major attractions to Christianity. Education, which was allied to Christianity, brought tremendous transformation of lives for individuals, families and communities in Nigeria, leaving lasting impressions and legacies, some of which have endured till date. In the words of Fuller, "when the missionary came to Africa, it was like one lighting a torchlight in a dark room" (Fuller, 181). Evangelism and social action have been criticized today, as lifting works, far above spirituality. This calls for a balance, namely; integrating the physical versus the spiritual. This is consistent with Jesus' teaching on the kingdom of God.

Christians today are still engaged in social ministry around the world. In Nigeria, such social ministry is still making impact and transforming lives. We have chosen the *Christian Rural and Urban Development Association of Nigeria* (CRUDAN), in order to illustrate this point.

Christian Rural and Urban Development Association of Nigeria (CRUDAN)

Christian Rural and Urban Development Association of Nigeria (CRUDAN) is a Christian non-governmental organization, that was formed in 1990 and its national headquarters is in Jos, Plateau State. The ultimate goal of

CRUDAN is to promote the kingdom of God, love, justice, righteousness and peace with God, one another and the environment (CRUDAN News Bulletin, 63).

CRUDAN sees the church as the primary agent of development (salt of the earth and light of the world), and a model kingdom community. It focuses on strategic Christian holistic development ministry for the restoration of creation as intended by God. Other areas of focus, includes participation of people, servant leadership, capacity building, stewardship and accountability, networking and collaboration, issues of equity and social justice and sustainability. CRUDAN's mission also includes promotion of Christian Development (Integral Mission), through advocacy with the church and member organizations, good governance, poverty reduction and transformation of the Nigerian society. Since 1990, CRUDAN has impacted Nigeria, through its vision and mission, and has transformed societies through its focus on provision of water, health services, leadership training, HIV/AIDS awareness seminars, and so on. Equally, playing closely related roles are Rural Christian Organization of Nigeria (RURCON), and Christian Health Association in Nigeria (CHAN), whose impacts have been enormous. These organizations and their activities have projected them, as playing the roles Jesus enjoined Christians to play; namely, of being 'salt' and 'light' to the world.

Conclusion

Jesus was a "contextualist" *par excellence*. He drew many of the illustrations in his teachings and parables from the typical natural Palestinian agrarian environment. They were familiar daily life experiences: of farmers sowing seeds, labourers in the vineyards, mustard seeds, yeast, tenants, fishersmen, wedding banquets, sheep and goats and so on. Jesus' use of these methods helped his hearers understand his teaching and consider carefully his applications.

Jesus decided to use the metaphors of "salt and light," because they were very familiar and popular to any Jew, and because they were consistent with Biblical reference or tradition in the OT and rabbinic sources. The message of Jesus was clear and easy to decode and to apply. Relaying Biblical truths to Christians today, requires uncomplicated, simple, and familiar metaphors, devoid of the high-flown, complicated and elitist messages that have characterized some Christian preachers in Nigeria. When a message is too complicated for people to comprehend and understand, the essence and meaning is removed from them. We need to refashion our messages by following Jesus' example, if we intend to reach the people who should be our target. We cannot effect any meaningful socio-religious, and indeed, any other form of transformation, when Christians have not understood the Biblical message, including its values, standards and application. Christians are called and are enjoined to make a difference in the world, to impact the world and to prevent and preserve it from moral decay and degeneracy, through Western values, and other forms of post-modernity.

Keller has noted that, when Jesus ministered, "he was in actual fact injecting salt into society. He wanted the character, conduct and compassion of his comrades to penetrate every part of the little world in which he and they lived" (951).

Keller indicates that for Christians to be able to effect any positive influence in the society, they like salt, must be applied, present, permeate, perform and impregnate the earth (951). He states:

> In the arts, science, in commerce, industry, in politics, in any area of human endeavour, we can be salt, with God working in us, both to will and do his own good pleasure; we are the potent salt which he expects us to be. We can be a source of health for our society (951).

Keller believes that this can be possible, through the transformation of Christian character that can slow the slide into subversive and destructive life styles (951). Keller, however, observes that it is not easy to impact the society. He states:

> It is not easy to do this. It is not easy to move and live counter to the current of corruption that flows so strongly in society. It is not easy to be different from those who drift with the crowd, who take the line of least resistance. It is not easy to take a tough stand against evil and injustice and exploitation. It is not easy to be scrupulously honest in business, industry, education or politics when others will not (951).

Keller seems to have captured the typical scenario that applies to the Nigerian nation as well. To transform the Nigerian society today of all its evils, requires radical policies and actions, with regard to those who are highly placed. Changing the values and standards, in the Nigerian life, requires radical decisions, in order to become the "light and salt" that Christians are really meant to be as Jesus enjoined in Matthew 5:13-16.

Being salt of the earth, implies that Christians exude qualities of faithfulness and truth, as well as righteousness that positively impact and influence society. These are qualities and standards that Jesus envisioned for true transformation to take place in a country like Nigeria. Being light of the world, involves illuminating the evil system and all forms of wickedness, that have characterized the Nigerian society, and not joining, as comrades, in promoting the evil decay and all forms of corruption. Christians in Nigeria, still hold the ace of not only leading the socio-religious transformation that Nigeria needs, but the one that can sustain the transformation and change that Nigeria desires at this moment.

CHAPTER 3

UNDERSTANDING PAUL'S CONTEXTUALIZATION METHODS FOR MISSION ENGAGEMENT IN AFRICA

I have made myself a slave to everyone, to win as many as possible. To the Jews I became like a Jew, to win the Jews. To those under the law I became like one under the law, so as to win those under the law… To the weak I became weak, to win the weak. I have become all things to all people so that by all possible means I might save some. I do all this for the sake of the gospel.

—1 Cor. 9:19-23 (NIV)

Introduction

The history of Christian mission is incomplete without the mention of Paul. Paul is considered in Christianity to be one of the greatest figures after Jesus Christ. Needham writes that, "more than any other individual, the apostle Paul was the man who made it possible for the Jesus movement to turn from being a purely Jewish sect into a largely Gentile body" (Needham, 49). Needham notes Paul's credentials as "supreme thinker and theologian of the early church," and concludes that, "next after Jesus Himself, Paul has had the greatest historical impact on the life and thought of the Christian church over the past 2000 years" (49). Bird has reinforced this assertion by stating that "Paul was the towering force behind much of early Christianity" (13). For Bird, "in the history of the Christian church, times of reformation and renewal have often found their catalyst in fresh encounters with the apostle," (13) and concludes that, "Paul, the servant of Jesus Christ, has a fresh word from God for the church in all ages" (13).

Without doubts, a discourse on mission today requires understanding Paul, as a quintessential Christian missionary *par excellence* and a missionary strategist for all time. Any contemporary reflection on mission will derive immeasurable insights from Paul's life, mission and its application.

Any understanding of Paul's contextualization methods for mission in today's Africa, is derived from the conviction that meaningful mission engagement in Africa today must take contextualization of the Gospel seriously. Contextualizing the Gospel entails the ability to proclaim and relate the Gospel message to the African soil, in a manner in which the Gospel speaks to the African heart, in order to make sense of African existential realities of life.

Mission historian Shenk states that one of the key features of contextualization is that, "it is a process whereby the Gospel message encounters a particular culture, calling forth a faith community which is culturally authentic and authentically Christian" (Shenk, 3). After identifying more than a dozen of Paul's mission strategies, Paul's contextualization methods are

chosen to meet the need of the moment. This chapter is based
on certain presuppositions that help to direct the flow of the
discourse.

i. Paul was the greatest Christian preacher and
    missionary agent apart from Jesus Christ.

ii. Paul's missionary strategies and impact are still
     relevant for mission in Africa today, and we need to
     appropriate Paul's vision and mission for the church.

iii. The contextualization approach to missions in
      Africa has been played down, and some
      (conservatives) "have traditionally been suspicious
      of contextualization" (Corrie online, 3).

iv. Modern challenges in mission call for an
     understanding of Paul's contextualization methods as
     the key to mission in Africa;

v. Contextualization is Biblical and imperative. Andrew
    Nkwalla has identified three reasons that portray
    contextualization as being imperative. These are the
    ministry of Christ, the example of the New Testament
    and the example of New Testament discipleship (3).

vi. The contextualization method provides safeguards
     against past errors of mission in Africa. David J.
     Hesselgrave corroborated this need with reference to
     mission in Africa indicating that it is a necessity (5).

In his *Pauline Theology and Mission Practice*, Gilliland has
asked whether Paul had a strategy. In answer to this puzzle,
Gilliland affirms that Paul had a strategy and that strategies

are necessary in missions (284). He defines strategy as something that has to do with the conception of a plan, before the campaign and its modification as the war progresses (284). Paul's style and mission methods strategically played significant roles. After identifying some "general features of Paul's missionary strategy" Gilliland, however, fails to mention Paul's contextual approach. However, McCain, in his *Notes on Acts of the Apostles*, discusses "Paul's missionary strategies" and shows how Paul was conscious of the context of his audience, where he contextualized his messages in the application of the gospel that he preached (McCain (d), 340-354).

Shoki Coe sees contextualization as the "missiological discernment of the signs of the times, seeing where God is at work and calling us to participate in it" (19). For Coe, contextualization is a missionary necessity as the Gospel moves from one cultural soil to another, and has to be translated, reinterpreted and expressed afresh in the new cultural soil (19).

By mission, we are referring to the proclamation of the Gospel of Jesus Christ (the *kerygma*) to the nations, in fulfillment of Jesus' command in Matthew 28:19:

> Therefore, go and make disciples of all nations, baptizing them in the name of the Father, and of the Son and of Holy Spirit, and teaching them to obey everything I have commanded you. And surely I am with you always, to the very end of the age (NIV).

Mission involves reaching out to the world, with the Gospel message of Jesus Christ. It involves discipleship and nurturing in faith. It is considered the "Great Commission," a mandate that God himself commanded, with all the assurances of Divine presence.

Stott sees the word "mission," as interchangeably used over the years with "witness" and "evangelism" (Stott, 15). For Stott, the "purpose of God's mission, the *missio Dei*, is the establishment of *Shalom* (Hebrew-peace)" (15). Mission is in the character of God as the "living God of the Bible is a sending God" (15). The Biblical concept of mission, is contextually conditioned and expressed within a particular milieu. Thus, Paul's model provides an example (paradigm) that could help to determine modern engagement of mission in Africa.

Paul and His Background

Scholarly works on Paul have presented him in many ways, and from various perspectives. Wright notes, "Paul in the twentieth century, has been used and abused much as in the first" (23). Brad H. Young corroborates Wright by stating that: "the question of how we use Paul for today remains as firmly on the table as ever" (60).

For example, Bird presents Paul as a persecutor, missionary, theologian, pastor and martyr (Bird, 15-28). Witherington III provides one portrait of Paul, referring to the "trinity of Paul's identity" namely, Paul the Jew, Paul the Roman citizen and Paul the Christian (18). We shall adopt his portrayal of Paul for the purpose of this chapter.

a.   **Paul the Jew**

Paul was a Jew. In Philippians 3:5, Paul stated:

If anyone else thinks he has reasons to put confidence in the flesh, "I have more: circumcised on the eighth day, of the people

> Israel, of the tribe of Benjamin, a Hebrew of
> Hebrews, in regard to the law, a Pharisee,
> as for zeal, persecuting the church, as for
> legalistic righteousness, faultless."

Paul refers to Jews as "my brothers, those of my own race, the people of Israel" (Rom. 9:3). Paul studied under Gamaliel in Jerusalem (Acts 22:3). Gamaliel was a grandmaster and teacher, who was greatly respected throughout the Jewish world. Gamaliel was a member of the Sanhedrin, the ruling body in Jerusalem and he greatly influenced Paul's theology (Young, 18). Paul was one who had advanced in Judaism beyond many Jews of his age and was extremely zealous for the traditions of the fathers (Gal. 1:14). It seems that Paul had a relative (a sister) in Jerusalem (Acts 23:16), and "the family of Paul seems to have had some influence in the city" (Young, 18). Paul also learned tent making from his father, which assisted him greatly later in his missionary career. Tarsus was noted for its leather goods, a cloth identified as cilicium, which came from the hair of black goats. This cloth was used to make tents (Getz, 12-13).

b. **Paul the Roman Citizen**

Acts 9:11 mentions that Paul (Saul) was from Tarsus which was a large, important Roman city and capital of the province of Celicia. It is described as not an "ordinary city" (Acts 21:39). Tarsus was a cosmopolitan city, a religious centre that blended all types of religious beliefs, philosophies and practices.

Here the worlds of the West, and of the East (oriental), met (Dibelius, 8). Tarsus was famous for its institutions, as it was considered the centre of learning in Asia Minor, comparable to Athens in Greece and Alexandria in Egypt. Getz adds that Tarsus was made *liberia civitas* (a free city), by the Romans in addition to its self-governing status (Getz, 13).

Tarsus was Paul's home (Acts 11:23, 22:3) and he was brought up there. Brad H. Young has added to some credentials of Tarsus thus:

> Indeed, Tarsus was no mean city. Connected to the Mediterranean Sea by the Cydnus River, it was strategically located, a thriving center of commerce, Greek culture and philosophic learning. The city had a university and was greatly influenced by the Stoic philosophic schools (14).

The educational status of Tarsus is buttressed further, when Strabo wrote:

> The people at Tarsus have devoted themselves so eagerly, not only to philosophy, but also to the whole round of education in general, that they had surpassed Athens, Alexandria or any other place that can be named where there have been schools and lectures of philosophers (Young, 15).

Acts 22:25 mentions Paul as a "Roman citizen." Acts 22:26, 28 also refer to his "citizenship." Paul, in reaction to his and Silas's imprisonment by the jailer in Philippi, told the Philippian officials wanting to quietly release them, "they beat us publicly without trial, even though we are Roman citizens" (Acts 16:37, 22:25, 28). Roman citizenship conferred certain benefits to its beneficiaries. For example Paul could appeal his case to Caesar, as a Roman citizen and while in prison, "was allowed to live by himself, with a soldier to guard him" (Acts 25:10-12; 28:16). Ben Witherington III writes:

> Paul's Roman citizenship would have provided him with advantages that would have assisted his work as a travelling evangelist. Besides having Roman justice on his side, he would have an instant entrée to any city in the Empire, especially Roman colony cities like Corinth or Philippi... He would have access to Roman roads and could travel with parties of other Roman citizens or even with Roman soldiers on a mission if need be. His positive interaction with the Praetorian guard while under house arrest (see Phil. 1) was no doubt in part because they were not disposed to ignore or despise a Roman citizen (73).

For Paul, the Greco-Roman world was his familiar terrain, and he was acquainted with the socio-political realities of the times. It also shaped Paul. Don Fleming accepts this observation, when he asserts, "Paul's style of systematic thinking suggests a Greek educational background of the type available in Tarsus" (Fleming, 427). In fact, it has been noted that, "Paul wrote Greek as if it were his mother language as his style was eloquent and classicist, possessing an extensive knowledge of Greek" (427). Thus, one could say that Paul was a product of a "globalized world," and he understood how to make use of the dynamics of such a multi-cultural world in his mission work, including his contextualization efforts. Dibelius captures this:

> It is unlikely that Paul would have become the great Christian missionary if his home had not been in this wider Judaism, if he had not been able to read and write Greek and possessed the Septuagint as his Bible, if he had not been used to accommodating himself to foreign customs, an eye for the wider world of highways by land and sea and for the great cities of the Mediterranean world (Dibelius, 22).

Early physical description of Paul is found in the apocryphal *Acts of Paul* as:

> A man of little stature, thin haired upon his head, crooked in the legs, of good state of body with eyebrows joining, and nose somewhat hooked, full of grace; for sometimes he appeared like a man, and sometimes he had the face of an angel (Young, 12).

c. **Paul the Christian**

Paul was also a Christian. Paul's dramatic and radical transformation, from a persecutor of the church to one who was destined to be persecuted for Jesus Christ is unprecedented in Christian history. Paul's encounter with Jesus Christ on the Damascus road changed his life. Later, Paul referred to the event as God's revelation (Gal. 1:16) and a moment in which he experienced God's grace and "apostleship to call people from among all the Gentiles" (Rom 1:5). Paul's Damascus event, changed his worldview and he experienced what Ben Witherington III refers to as a "thorough resocialization" (77). At the Damascus encounter, Paul was called and commissioned as a "chosen instrument to carry my name before the Gentiles" (Acts 9:15). Paul's vision about God was changed, and his mission redirected. A former zealot of the law and persecutor of the church was now destined to be zealous for Christ and to be persecuted (Acts 9:16). Getz notes that Paul's life was dramatically changed by the power of the Holy Spirit and he was born again (31). Paul's conversion remained a pivotal event, and a constant reminder throughout his ministry, shaping his theological thoughts in respect of the law, the grace of God, salvation, the righteousness of God and of justification by faith. "His transformation is unequalled in the history of Christianity" (Getz, 31).

Paul was commissioned to the Gentiles (Act 9:5). Paul also spoke of receiving God's grace "to be a minister of Christ Jesus to the Gentiles" (Rom. 15.16). The term, Gentiles, was taken from the Hebrew *goyim* (Greek *ethne* or *Hellenes*), and originally referred to "nations" before it acquired a restricted use (Blair, 403). It was used to refer to all non-Israelite people (Gal. 2:15). Israel was prohibited from copying the "detestable ways" of the Gentiles (Deut. 18:9), who had a reputation for not knowing God, being selfish, immoral, greedy, ungodly and idolatrous (Matt. 6:32; Rom 1:18-22, Eph. 4:17-19). In fact, "in the eyes of the Jews, Gentiles had no hope of salvation, because they were excluded from the covenant promises that God gave Israel (Eph. 2:11-12)" (Fleming, 148).

In the chapter, we shall refer to Paul's missionary activity at Athens where Paul "gave a conspicuous exhibition of his marvelous versatility" (Meyer, 118) as a missionary. Meyer notes that:

> No ordinary Jew could have entered so thoroughly into the spirit of the place as did the great apostle or excited sufficient interest among its philosophers to justify their calling a special assembly of the council of the Aeropagus to hear a full statement of the new teaching he brought to their ears (Mayer, 118).

It also brings out the passage as "a brilliant example of missionary strategy" (Hall, 101). Dean Flemming sees "Paul's address to the Athenians in Acts 17 as perhaps the outstanding example of intercultural evangelistic witness in the New Testament" (72).

Paul in Athens (Acts 17:16-34)

Paul visited Athens on his second missionary journey. Paul had visited Thessalonica and Berea, where he preached the Gospel and some believed the message with "great eagerness" (17:11). Athens was famous for its culture, home of great dramatists, and of great philosophers, like Plato and Aristotle. Athens was the most famous, among the university cities like Tarsus and Alexandria (Hall, 101). Bruce calls it the "mother of Western civilization" (1298) and "a city notorious for its liking for intellectual chat" (Bruce, 1298). Meyer refers also to the *educated literati* of Athens (120).

Athens was a city of antiquity exhibiting rich historical monuments and legacies. It was a city rich in art, architecture, literature and politics from the golden age of Greek history (5th Century B.C). Meyer notes, "on every side were achievements of human genius. Temples that Phidias had designed; statues that Praxiteles had wrought" (117). Philo, the Jewish Hellenist historian also spoke of the Athenians, who "were the keenest-sighted mentally of the Greeks, famous for their temples, statues and monuments." Appollonius, the philosopher and contemporary of Paul, rebuked them for their lascivious jigs at the festivals of Dionysius and for the love of human slaughter in the gladiatorial games (Hall, 102). They were lovers of pleasure and of novelty (Acts 17:21). "Though religious, their spiritual level was not exceptionally high." (101) Athens was a *citas foederata* (a city linked to Rome by treaty). It was a city that was renowned.

Paul came to this city and was "distressed that the city was full of idols" (v. 16). Paul met with the Jews and God-fearing Greeks in the synagogue and in the market place daily and

"reasoned" with them. He debated with Epicureans and Stoic
philosophers, who had a low view of God, about the world and
the hereafter. He preached about Jesus and the resurrection,
and they accused him of speaking nonsense. Some thought
that he was advocating foreign gods and therefore called him a
"babbler" (v. 18). They decided to bring him to the Areopagus.

The Areopagus was an ancient and highly respected
council of philosophers in Athens, situated on Mars Hill.
They were responsible for the orderly conduct of public
lecturing in Athens (Fleming, 28). Paul was invited to the
Areopagus to explain more of the "new teaching" that he was
presenting. It was then that Paul stood up and addressed the
Athenians gathered at the Areopagus to listen to him. Here,
Paul showed his best in his masterly, powerful, spellbinding
address. It was a unique address, "full of grace, intellectual
sequence, grandeur of conception and range, stately march of
eloquent words" (Meyer, 118). Paul spoke of their external
religiousness (evident everywhere), in reference to the altar
that had an inscription, "to an unknown God." He said, "I see
that in every way you are very religious" (v.22). This became
the core of Paul's contextualization message where he used
it to draw their attention to God who could be known and
who had indeed revealed himself in history (cf Rom. 1:20).
He alluded to some of their poets, in order to build a bridge
between them.

He called for them to respond by repenting from their
"ignorance" (v. 30). However, when they heard of the mention
of the resurrection of the dead, some of them sneered, while
others said, "we want to hear you again on this subject"
(v. 32). Some who became followers of Paul believed. For

example, Dionysius, a member of the Areopagus, and Damaris and others. Keener maintains that the conversion of Dionysius was significant as he was a member of the Areopagus, writing that, "although Paul's message to the university community of his day did not produce massive immediate results, his ministry to the Areopagus is clearly effective" (374).

Contextualizing Acts 17:16-34 to Mission in Africa Today

Paul's ministry in Athens has attracted scholarly responses discussing how his contextualization message can be applied to modern mission engagement in Africa.

David A. Reed has noted that, "Africans have written many studies on the subject of the Areopagus speech" (97). We will put some highlights on Paul's Athenian address here:

i. Similarities between religious Athenians and the African traditional religious heritage. Paul encountered Athenians who he described as "very religious" (v. 22). The vast presence of shrines and altars show that Athens was indeed, religiously committed to idols. According to Reed, "the presence of the numerous idols apparently contradicted his perception of Athens as the cultural and intellectual center of the ancient world" (Reed, 92).

    Mbiti has described Africans as "notoriously religious," and that religion permeates all aspects of the African life. According to Mbiti, "African peoples do not know how to exist without religion," (1-3) and asserts that Africans had no atheists in the true sense of the word. To Ehusani,

> . . . this all-pervading sense of the sacred, a unique African legacy, is a gift to Christianity. Missionary Christianity has nothing to add to the African spiritual worldviews, but it rather has a lot to gain from it (208).

God's consciousness in Africa is reflective in their knowledge of Him, through theophoric names, attributes of Him, and in proverbs. Ikenga Metuh observed also that there is a paradox of transcendence, and immanence of God in African religions, which is not peculiar to Africans (59).

Because God is considered as a *deus incertus deus remotus*; that is, "remote and a withdrawn God," He is not worshipped in most African societies, not even in images of Him in drawings or carvings, though there are a few exceptions of this in some parts of Igbo land, Ashanti, Dogon and Ambo (Metuh, 47). According to Taylor, "He is God whom man has made in his own image" (67).

Reflecting on Acts 17:16-34, with reference to African traditional religion, Oleka remarks that:

> It is a remarkable fact that people from a background of African traditional religion respond more readily to the Gospel than people from a different religious background, say Buddhism. One possible explanation is that the limited knowledge of God in African traditional religion has some common points

> with the full revelation of God in Christ for a
> point of contact. African traditional religion
> shows God as creator, spirit, transcendent
> and all-powerful. When the Gospel preaches
> the love, grace and mercy of God in Jesus
> Christ, His God who is far off becomes the
> God who is near (Jer. 23:23) (130).

It is Oleka's conviction that African traditional religion has areas of contact with the Biblical concepts of God and his revelation that makes the proclamation of the gospel in this context easier, more familiar and meaningful. Paul Mumo Kisau corroborates Oleka by showing that:

> Like the Athenians, Africans are very
> religious and have numerous shrines. The
> concept of the supreme God in African
> traditional religion is also shadowy, not
> unlike the concept that led to the erection of
> an altar to the unknown God (1331).

As a missionary in Africa, Richard Gehman has realized this African reality writing, "knowledge of the Supreme Being, the creator of heaven and earth, was a valuable heritage of traditional Africa" (174). Gehman points out that Africans even had the knowledge of Paradise Lost (174-176), and concludes that,

> . . .it has become quite clear that the grace
> of God has been at work in the hearts of the
> African before the coming of missionaries.
> This measure of truth known to the African

has served as a road for the gospel to enter into the hearts of the peoples' (Gehman, 84-86).

What Gehman identifies as elements of the "Grace of God," "measure of truth," and the "road to the gospel" is what has been considered among others as elements in African worldviews that are *praeparatio evangelica*, that is, preparatory grounds for the spread of the gospel.

ii. Paul was constructive and corrective in his mission at Athens. Dean Flemming has shown how Paul was able to lead the Athenians to the knowledge of the true God, through "various apologetic arguments in verses 24-29" and constructively corrected their notions of God (Flemming, 76-77). Missions today must, constructively, engage African worldviews, in order to correct some of what Richard J. Gehman calls, "errors in ATR," such as Africa's concept of the remote God and idolatry (84-86).

iii. Paul preached to the Athenians in their language (Greek) and they understood him well. Using rhetoric, the system of argument and reasoning prized by educated people of the day, he clearly communicated the Gospel in a way that people could understand and follow. Missions today must seek to communicate in a language that speaks to the hearts of the people. Early Christian missionaries in Africa tried in this area, and early translation efforts of some

African languages and the Bible remains the pioneer work of missionaries (Sanneh, 28-31).

iv. Athenians heard something new in Paul's address (v. 19). Africans, generally, are very receptive to new ideas. The Gospel message must carry good news, which is new and attractive. Contemporary news coverage of Africa has been consistently negative. Most news, that comes from Africa focuses on hunger, crises and wars, environmental degregadation, corruption, illiteracy and the effects of poverty. The Gospel message has the potential to present good news, which is refreshing and empowering to Africans.

v. Paul "reasoned" daily with the Athenians. He interacted with them, identified with them, presented the Gospel to them and answered their questions. Paul met the Jews in the synagogue, which was their familiar terrain, and some God-fearing Jews in a market place, in their relaxed environment. Paul met his target audience at their convenient places. They were religious people, but they needed a greater knowledge of God. The Gospel in Africa today must meet people wherever they are found, with the sole aim of presenting something new to them. There is the need for an alternative message that will interest people's ears and hearts.

vi. Paul was scorned (v. 32). They called him a "babbler" (v 18). To scorn someone is to condemn, sneer or scoff at someone (Dictionary and Thesaurus, 665).

To call someone a "babbler" is to insult one, who is incoherent in talk or is a mere chatterer. These forms of insult and contempt greeted Paul's mission in Athens. Later, Paul referred to similar mission experiences in 2 Corinthians 6:4, where he listed other experiences such as:

> Great endurance in trouble, hardships, and distresses, in beatings, imprisonment and riots, sleepless nights and hunger, in the Holy Spirit, in truthful speech, and in the power of God, with weapons of righteousness, through glory and dishonour, bad report and good report, genuine, yet regarded as impostors, known, yet regarded as unknown, dying, and yet we live on, beaten and yet not killed, poor, yet making many rich, having nothing and possessing everything (paraphrased).

This passage summarizes Paul as a quintessential missionary, who had adapted himself to all situations in "order to win some."

vii. Paul delivered a sound message. His address about the living God in Athens was profound and theologically sound. It was also unambiguous. He caught the attention of Athenians who heard him. Luke, the writer of Acts, did not indicate that Paul was faulted in his speech on theological grounds, but, rather, they responded differently, "we will hear him again on this" (v. 32). As the Gospel message is proclaimed in Africa today, the message must be very clear, unambiguous and relevant to issues that concern Africans. Olabimtan has identified such issues, as "areas of this global reality that must inform mission at this stage of human history," such as governance, globalization, poverty, burgeoning population growth, migration and multiculturalism, rapid urbanization, environmental crises, culture change, religious and ethnic tension, and the challenge of new morality (Olabimtan, 83-87).

viii. Paul did not outrightly condemn Athenians of idol worship; but he commended them for being "very religious in every way" (v. 22). He took them from the "unknown" to the "known," as he presented God to them. Mission today in Africa must learn to respect and love Africa, its peoples, culture, history, and beliefs, before it can reach them with the Gospel whose central tenet is the love of God to all men. Paul was not chased away in Athens, because he respected the Athenians. That was why Paul's audience listened carefully to what he had to say. Mission needs listening ears. Africans are good listeners, and as story lovers, the Gospel comes readily to a people whose worldview fits in very appropriately. Paul constructively engaged them and led them to the truth. Mission in Africa today must avoid prejudices, biases and the superior outlook of the Western European type, which characterized past missionary endeavour in some parts of Africa.

ix. Paul delivered his speech with power and mastery. Mission in Africa today needs to engage Africans with the gospel of power to a people, who are "power conscious." Charles Kraft, a past missionary to Africa, C.G. Bäeta, G.C. Oosthuisen and J.S. Trimingham have emphasised this as a necessary requirement in mission in Africa in order to avoid the errors of the past missionary encounter (Gwamna, 72-73). Pentecostal growth in Africa today should provide the stimulus for this re-discovery.

x. Paul challenged the Athenians concerning repentance, judgment and the last day. His message was centered on core aspects of salvation, faith, justification and the grace of God. Missions today must engage Africa with the message of salvation and the true essence of the kerygma, and not the "butter and bread" prosperity Gospel, that has become very fashionable among some preachers.

xi. Paul did not compromise his Christian message to the Athenians. Flemming notes this when he writes that: "Paul is able to convey biblical revelation in the language and categories of his Greek listeners without, as N.T. Wright puts it, 'travelling down the slippery slope towards syncretism'" (77). As had been noted earlier, one of the suspicions and fears of contextualization by some today is that it leads to syncretism. Nevertheless, if we follow Paul, contextualization can be insulated from syncretism. Contextualization must not compromise cultural worldviews in order to reach people. Contextualization can penetrate the cultural worldview of a people, as we have already seen, in order to "correct" or "transform" it without giving in to syncretistic trappings of culture, particularly, in Africa, where culture is a potent force in most societies.

xii. Though the response was little in Athens (part of a typical mission experience), a seed of the gospel was sown. Keener has noted this earlier. It left imprints among philosophers, who heard him in Athens. Similarly, the Gospel must leave imprints in Africa wherever it is preached.

xiii. Paul identified and interacted with the groups he met in Athens: Jews, God-fearing Greeks and philosophers. He was involved in cross-cultural mission. Paul was able to relate with them at their levels, because he was able to adapt to them, despite their diversities, beliefs and peculiarities. Today, Africa is no more the "Dark Continent" of the nineteenth century. Globalization has opened the villages to the satellite televisions and the mass media is an added boost to the influence of multi-ethnic consciousness and reality in Africa. Mission engagement in Africa must recognize this reality and shift its paradigm to fit its relevance to its mission goal.

Conclusion

Paul was a great strategist in missions. As we stated earlier, Paul had other mission models that contributed immensely to his successes in mission. Most of such strategies were adopted, as a result of Paul's contextualization efforts. For example, Paul's use of letters were written to meet specific needs of church congregations, and to address practical issues of some congregations, as was the case with the Epistles to the Corinthians, Galatians and Thessalonians among others. E. Randolph Richards has provided a hint that Paul was able to maximize letter writing in his ministry, because of the ease of travel within the Mediterranean shores, and a courier culture was very popular (189). Richards gives details of ship travel in ancient Mediterranean world at the time of Paul, which helps to contextualize Paul's mission (190).

Paul showed commitment and brought his intellectual capabilities to bear on his mission practice. It eased his work and enhanced effectiveness. Such commitment of talented people is needed in missions in Africa, in order to be able to make the kind of impact Paul made. Added to his multi-cultural upbringing, Paul's commissioning to the Gentile mission kept his focus on the Gospel message (2 Cor. 4:2, 17).

Other models, such as Paul's focus on urban ministry, collaboration in mission, tent-making, friendship in mission, and discipleship (follow up), are models that require or need to be explored, and adopted for effective mission engagement in Africa. However, it must be warned that particular contexts determine the applicability, or otherwise, of a strategy in mission, hence the flexibility and adaptivity in mission as was exemplified by Paul becomes relevant.

Africa is still groping today in sin, illiteracy, poverty, civil unrests, underdevelopment, corruption and all the negative indices of civilized cultures. Only the Gospel of Jesus Christ can reverse the African condition. The Gospel, which is the good news, must be proclaimed in Africa, just as Jesus declared, namely "to preach good news to the poor, proclaim freedom to the prisoners, and recovery of sight to the blind, to release the oppressed, and to proclaim the year of the Lord's favor" (Lk. 4:18-19). This can be achieved today, only, through purposeful mission engagement in Africa.

CHAPTER 4

PENTECOSTAL PHENOMENON AND GROWTH IN NIGERIA

Introduction

Nigeria has witnessed the rise and growth of Pentecostalism. It is a major player in the shift of global Christianity to the south. According to Gyadu, "Pentecostalism is the area in which the growth in African Christianity has been most conspicuous" (10). To Barrett, the Pentecostal rise is "the main and major sign and wonder of our time" (Gyadu, 15). Pentecostal experience around the world today, and particularly in Nigeria, is part of the resurgence of religion in the twenty-first century and is a challenge to post-modernist speculations about the demise of religion. It also fulfils the projections by David Barrett, Philip Jenkins, Andrew Walls, and Walter J. Hollenweger of the prophetic role Africa will play in global Christianity. Walls had written about a "major recession from Christianity and a major accession to it" (118): recession in the Western so-called "missionized" world and accession in the "southern continents" of Asia, Latin America, and the two-thirds world. Walls concluded that, "at the end of the twentieth century, Africa was appearing as the Christian heartland" (118).

In fact, Hollenweger predicted that, "by the beginning of the twenty-first century, Pentecostal Christians were expected to number as many as all other Protestants put together" (Gyadu, 15). Miller has provided a significant hint in respect of the global spread of Pentecostalism noting:

> Given the somewhat amorphous character of Pentecostal and charismatic Christianity, it is difficult to know how many people fit this classification, but most estimates put the number of renewalists at more than 500 million, or about a quarter of the total Christian population. It is widely regarded as the fastest growing element of Christianity and, as a consequence, it is reshaping the demography of Christianity, with the majority of Christians now living in the Southern Hemisphere rather than in Europe or North America (Miller, 9).

Illustrating this point further, Miller stated that:

> Pentecostal and charismatic Christian churches, many of which have no connection to North American missionary activity, are fueling the growth of Christianity. For example, the Redeemed Christian Church of God (RCCG), which started in Nigeria, is now in 60 countries in Africa, the United States, Europe, and parts of Asia and the Middle East. In Nigeria alone it has 2,000 congregations. The RCCG holds an annual convention attended by several million of people: the largest meeting of Christians in the world (Miller, 10).

The above indication, by Miller points to the significant role of Nigeria and its large Christian population as a potential resource, in shaping African Christianity. Contextualizing this fact further, Anderson stated that:

> Countries like South Korea, Nigeria, Brazil, and India have become major Christian missionary-sending nations, many of whose missionaries are Pentecostal. Half of the world's Christians today live in developing, poor countries, where forms of Christianity are very different from those of Western Christianity. These Christians have been profoundly affected by several factors, including the desire to have a more contextual and culturally relevant form of Christianity, the rise of nationalism, a reaction to what are perceived as "colonial," and foreign forms of Christianity, and the burgeoning charismatic renewal (30).

Some see the Pentecostal phenomenon, as a "new Pentecost" and the outpouring of the Holy Spirit to all nations, "re-awakening," and "religion made to travel." For Cox, it is a "recovery of primal spirituality" (Gyadu, 15). Marshall refers to it as the "Pentecostal revolution" (19) and according to Anderson it is the "African Reformation" (19). Pentecostalism, in Nigeria, presents a variety of features, beliefs and practices, which make its categorization complex and difficult. Adogame rightly observed that, "the criteria for categorizing these movements as Pentecostal or charismatic can be confusing" (185). He states further that:

> By all accounts, Pentecostalism and related charismatic movements represent one of the fastest growing segments of global Christianity. At least a quarter of the world's two billion Christians are thought to be members of these lively, highly personal faiths, which emphasize such spiritually renewing 'gifts of the Spirit'

as speaking in tongues, divine healing and prophesying (Adogame, 186).

In fact, Pentecostal and Charismatic Studies Research in Nigeria, shows that the complexity of caterogization of these movements could be a tedious task as distinct features overlap between them (Gaiya, 1).

Since the Pentecostal wave started, as a major form of Christian experience in the 1970s till date, it has attracted more followership and focus. Within this context, however, Nigeria has emerged as a leading Pentecostal nation in Africa and is expected to lead in world Christianity. Marshall puts it this way:

> Nigeria has been the site of Pentecostalism's greatest explosion on the African continent, and the movement's extra-ordinary growth shows no signs of slowing. A marginal current within Nigeria Christianity in the early 1970s, by the turn of the millennium had become its overwhelmingly dominant form, counting tens of millions of adherents, and powerfully influencing Christian practice and doctrines across all denominations (19).

The rise and growth of Pentecostalism in Nigeria has been documented by, Ogbu Kalu, Richard Burgess, Ruth Marshall, Matthews A. Ojo, and Donatus Pius Ukpong, among others. These works have shown how several factors, have contributed to the development of Pentecostalism today and the impact on African Christianity as a whole. Richard Flory and Kimon H. Sargeant have posed three questions that are of significance and relevant to this chapter. First, how are we to make sense of the varieties of Pentecostal experience and expression in the modern world? Second, what is fueling this diverse movement's growth? Third, what is the implication of its growth, not only for sociological theories about religion and its continued role in societies around the world, but also for understanding the role that Pentecostalism and religion, in general, may be playing in the life of modernizing secular societies? (Magbadelo, 15).

Understanding Pentecostal Rise and Growth in Nigeria

1. Pentecostals' negative perception of mainline churches. One of the main reasons why Pentecostalism in Nigeria has drawn a large number of followers is the negative perception of the mainline churches by Christians and non-Christians alike. Such perceptions include accusing the mainline churches of being "dead churches," docile, too quiet and rigid in their enforcement of standards (Adeleye, 21). The "rush" to new Pentecostal churches reflects the need for a new experience that is livelier and where the presence of the Holy Spirit is felt. Thus, new patterns that have developed to buttress this point further lie behind the large exodus to, or subtle identification with, Pentecostal churches and ministries. For example in Jos, God's Grace Ministry, led by Rev. Danjuma Goshwe Fwenji (a COCIN pastor), and Evangelical Bible Outreach Ministry International (EBOMI) led by Prophet Isa El-Buba, have attracted large crowds.

Programmes of the Church of Eternal Life and their night vigils under the leadership of Pastor Academe are also one of the major crowd-pullers in Jos. This is similar to the Throne Room Trust Ministry programmes in Kafanchan, led by Pastor Emmanuel Kure.

In most cases, members of these ministries and churches maintain dual membership; that is, they maintain partly Pentecostal and mainline affiliations. Many of such members would prefer to play it safe, not being ready to confront, or raise complaints and their dislikes within the mainline churches. They are equally, comfortable attending programmes of a Pentecostal nature, because of their messages, programmes and lively sessions.

2. The lure of the crowd. Today we live in an age where the crowd easily influences people's unthinking preferences. The trend of the "pop culture" influenced by the mood of the crowd has been evident in various facets of Nigerian life, including the religious sphere. We have people today who are easily carried away by where the crowd is. They flock there to hear what they want to hear. In other words, they are men and women with "itching ears,"

> . . . a people who are like infants, who are tossed back and forth by the waves, and blown here and there by every wind of teaching and by the cunning and craftiness of men in their deceitful scheming (Eph. 4:14).

The effects of the flow towards such churches, is what Adeleye has also highlighted when he writes that, "some of this new generation of Christians have turned the grace of God into a license for all manner of unrighteousness." They produce a new generation of Sadducees whom he calls "happisees," the new Epicureans, who are the pleasure lovers and easy-going Christians of our day (Adeleye, 21).

3.   Proliferation of campus fellowships. Modern day Pentecostalism owes a great deal to the role university campuses and students played in its birth, nurture and growth. Scholarly works by Ogbu Kalu, Matthews Ojo, and Richard Burgess, have shown how Pastor William Kumuyi, the General Overseer of the Deeper Life Bible Church, Pastor E. Adeboye of the Redeemed Christian Church of God, and others, started from the university campuses. The university campus provided an ideal environment as the nucleus and incubating grounds of Nigerian Pentecostalism. This trend has continued with greater momentum in Nigerian higher institutions today. Most campus fellowships today draw membership from both mainline churches and Pentecostal ones. They have continued the split or balkanization of denominationally-based churches and ministries. In fact, some of the leaders and co-ordinators of such groups see themselves, as potential founders and overseers of their prospective churches in future.

Offiong captures the mood of the youths this way:

> Youths now see themselves as being anointed by the Holy Spirit to serve God as pastors and in other capacities in their own establishments, instead of going through the bureaucratic procedure in the historic churches. Thus, leadership ambition has partly contributed to the emergence and growth of Pentecostalism in Nigeria (136).

Though the proliferation of campus fellowship groups is perceived as having a positive impact on the growth of Pentecostalism in Nigeria, it has led to clashes between non-Christians (Muslims particularly), who see them as disturbing their studies by their use of loudspeakers at fellowship hours and in classrooms which are meant for academic endeavours. The very unrestrained provocative sermons have also caused protests and clashes between Christian and Muslim students. Campus fellowship groups have also been criticized for diverting students' attention from studies to religious activities without striking a balance towards academic performance in the search for spirituality.

4. The lure of popular theology. Popular theology is a theology that is spread by half-baked theologians in Christian ministry. It is a theology of the market place as everyone propagates it. It is a freelance theology that lacks serious and sound biblical hermeneutics. It is a theology of the people.

Preachers and leaders who are not well trained theologically characterise Pentecostalism in Nigeria today. They have promoted a popular and cheap Christian message, manipulating and distorting the Gospel. This could explain why a lot of preaching and teaching in Pentecostal churches today lacks a Biblical base, and serves only to confuse and lead astray.

5. Emotional Appeal. One of the trademarks of Pentecostal and Charismatic churches is that their services are usually emotional, enthusiastic and loud. Some of them use electronic gadgets such as loudspeakers, musical instruments and computerized equipment that easily draw crowds. These appeal to the youth and have drawn many of them to the Pentecostal fold. Adedeji has shown how musical styles have found their way into the Nigerian music scene with radical brands of gospel music such as Gospel reggae, Gospel waka, Gospel-fuji, juju Gospel, Gospel rap, Gospel raga, gos-pop, makossa-Gospel and Gospel rock (237).

These singers, among others, have been able to Christianize and contextualize some secular musical tunes and lyrics into Christian-based ones, and have drawn many to Pentecostal churches. The role of musical concerts and availability of Euro-American gospel CDs and VCDs, such as the music of Kirk Franklin, Ron Kenoly, Don Moen, Fred Hammond, Donnie McClulin and Cece Winas, "are sold in many

Pentecostal music shops in the country" (Effiong, 137).

Closely related to the music role and attraction, are the loud and highly charged emotional services that have replaced the quiet, solemn traditional church services. Commenting on this phenomenon, Asaju notes that, "the trademark of new Pentecostal and Charismatic churches is in fact the noisy pattern of praise and worship which enhances dance, dispelling of gloom and stress, making for likely service" (107). Asaju notes further that even the prayers are designed, "to be shouted aloud in a repetitive, combatant and aggressive manner against perceived spiritual enemies" (104). He sees the noise pattern, as a trademark of being "living," "active," "anointed," "Holy Spirit filled" and "born again" (Asaju, 104). The noise and dance sessions have also infiltrated into some mainline churches, to the extent that distinguishing them, based on form of worship today, could be very difficult.

Asaju and others have noted the cathartic effect of such expressions, which address present socio-economic realities of Nigerians.

6. Socio-economic factors: One of the recurring factors that has been identified and stressed, as a major feature towards Pentecostalism in Nigeria are the socio-economic and political conditions in Nigeria. The Pentecostal churches, witnessed a rapid rise and growth in the 1980s at the same time as Nigeria's economic fortunes experienced severe setbacks and

a slide in performance. The oil revenue had fallen, which resulted in the introduction of the Structural Adjustment Programme (SAP) and other World Bank induced economic policies. This was compounded, by the Nigerian ruling elite's corruption over a number of years. Unemployment grew substantially accompanied by strikes and other forms of protests amidst frustration and mass discontentment. Crime also increased as poverty became a common daily experience. Magbadelo captures this scenario thus:

> The progressive expansion of poverty, ignorance, hunger, disease, unemployment, exploitation, alienation, oppression and dispossession in Nigeria since independence has continued to influence the resort of Nigerians to a search for the spiritual essence of their being. The socio economic and political adversaries in the country provide a fertile ground for the planting, germination, growth and balkanization of all forms of religion (22).

Pentecostalism is believed to have provided a platform for people to fill the vacuum that had been created because of the state's failure to provide safety and fulfill its own social contract in providing for the welfare of the people. It has provided grounds for people to express themselves, their frustrations and their hopes. It also provides assurances of a better tomorrow – a theme which Pentecostal messages stress under different names and programs. This partly explains the change in emphasis and focus of Pentecostal messages from the 1980s on holiness to prosperity, which has now drawn more people to it. It also indicates the dynamic interplay of the factors that shape the conditions for persistent attraction to Pentecostalism.

7. Elite Dimension. There is the elite dimension to the pull towards Pentecostalism in Nigeria. As earlier noted, Pentecostalism developed and grew within the university environment. It produced an educated elite that has influenced its spread and growth till date. Such leaders and preachers still provide the lead and attraction to Pentecostal churches. Elaborating on this, Magbadelo writes that, "their style of language use, phonetics, dressing and mien portray them, at face value, as the epitome of modernity and decency, a major attraction to the youth and university students" (22). Examples of such factors who have influenced membership through their eloquence include Pastor Chris Oyakhilome of Christ Embassy Church, Pastor Chris Okotie of Household of God Church, Lagos, Pastor Tunde Bakare of the Latter Rain Assembly, Lagos and Pastor Paul Enenche of Dunamis International Gospel Center, Abuja, among others. Their charisma, power of speech and communication skills are qualities that have drawn a large following. "They are effervescent orators radiating with an audacious air of sophistic condition" (Magbadelo, 22). Reuben Abati has been quoted on this further:

> The new generation pastor is a spell-binder;
> he dresses well; he rides very flashy cars; he
> even carries a gun, just in case. He is a part-
> time businessman. He doesn't need to have
> attended any Bible college. As long as he can
> quote passages from the Bible and report to
> a bewildered congregation about what his
> Daddy told him in the night, he would get a
> captive audience (Magbadelo, 22).

Thus, it can be said that while this may be an attraction of some elite to such churches, it has unconsciously created some resentful feelings and consciousness that are prevalent in Nigeria today.

8. Attraction of external linkages. It is the assumption of some Nigerians that exposure to oversea countries, such as the United States of America and Europe, opens a flood gate for unconditional and unlimited opportunities of greener pastures, that offer better jobs, better pay and so on.

Pentecostalism is linked to external linkages, as their leaders are believed to have such external connections and could attract such favours and opportunities. This thinking has led to a "mad chase" by pastors and members, who seek travel visas and identification with some Pentecostal churches in order to travel out. That such opportunities possibly exist are a major attraction to young graduates, who believe that they could rise within Pentecostal circles to enjoy such opportunities.

9.   Search for quick and immediate solutions. One of the reasons that has been identified for the rush towards Pentecostalism is the search, by Nigerians, for quick results to their problems. This derives from the fact that Pentecostals are believed to provide solutions to problems, through their powerful prayers (both for breaking of curses and covenants, and against demonic attacks and other forms of satanic bondage), as is characteristic of the Mountain of Fire and Miracles Ministry (MFM). Thus, "anointed men of God," and churches are identified and patronized, through visits to their churches and programs. The massive annual attendances in some of these churches includes, the Shiloh annual gathering of the Living Faith Church at Canaan Land, Ota; the Annual Holy Ghost Congress of the Redeemed Christian Church of God along Ibadan-Lagos road; and of the Deeper Life Bible Church. Others include, The Lord's Chosen Charismatic Revival Ministries; Synagogue Church of All Nations; and Annual Bethel Convention of the Dominion International Chapel. In fact, the response and the rush to these programs has reached the level of an "explosion," a "mad rush" or "a new Pentecost." Reflecting on this, Adewole noted that:

> The search for quick and immediate solutions to problems . . . could be seen in the mad rush by Nigerian Christians to any form of gathering where all sorts of miracles are advertised. The reason for this mad rush is not far-fetched, for Nigerian Christians are

> bedeviled by a myriad of socio-economic problems. . . For many Nigerian Christians, the Gospel makes sense only to the extent that it promises to deliver them from material and social forces that constitute the untold yet avoidable hardships of daily survival. . . God is seen as God only when he answers prayers here and now, and provides immediate solutions to the problems faced by his children (52).

10. Bread and butter factor. Some have been attracted to Pentecostalism due to their expectations of what material benefits they could get. Their focus is on the benefits they could derive from some social ministries. These include provisions of food; attention to widows, the poor and orphans; empowerment programs; scholarships; loans; water supply, medical services and payment of other bills. Just as in Jesus' day, many have been attracted to Pentecostalism because of what they can get to meet their physical needs. Jesus had noted this in his ministry when he said, "I tell you the truth, you are looking for me, not because you saw miraculous signs but because you ate the loaves and had your fill" (Jn. 2:26). For example, the feeding program of the Guiding Light Assembly, Lagos, among the people in Obalande, through the "Obalande, Project" attracts people to the church and continues to draw much commendation among inhabitants in Obalande.

These Pentecostal churches have provided for physical needs, through their engagement in social ministries and in turn, have received commendations and massive following. The "bread and butter" approach, though not the sole aim of social ministries by some of these churches, has incidentally drawn people to them.

Pentecostalism, in Nigeria, has been known to exhibit characteristics reminiscent of the early apostolic church. Acts 2:42-47 says that early believers devoted themselves to teaching, fellowship, breaking of bread and to prayer. "Every one was filled with awe, and many wonders and miraculous signs were done by the apostles" (2:43). The early church exhibited the love, care and character of a Holy Spirit church. Pentecostalism today is a replica of the early church. As they care and extend love to others through social ministries, they have increased membership to unprecedented heights. Examples of this assertion are evident in some churches such as Family Worship Centre, Abuja, Dunamis Church Abuja, Dominion International Chapel, Abuja, and The Apostolic Church, Lagos, among others. For some it forms the basis for practicalizing the prosperity gospel message.

Social ministries within some of these Pentecostal churches have focused on aspects that touch on the people's socio-economic realities, thereby meeting the needs of the people. This also helps to confirm the assertion that one of the reasons for the attraction to Pentecostalism is this meeting of people's needs. Anderson similarly stated this, when he noted that the emergence of Pentecostalism today, indicates that there are unresolved questions and problems facing the church in Africa that will remain a major challenge for Pentecostal churches to address (56). The confrontation of some of these issues and concerns brings out the relevance of Pentecostalism in Nigeria. It also fits into the model of Gyadu's "salvation as transformation and empowerment," and other concerns that he has espoused in his work (17).

11. Pentecostalism, women involvement and empowerment. Women have been particularly drawn to Pentecostalism, because it has provided them uninhibited religious space (against African patriarchal inhibitions) for greater participation and empowerment. Pentecostalism has provided opportunities for women to aspire and attain leadership roles and they have assumed more visible roles than in the mainline churches. Some of the women have taken up leadership of churches after the death of their husbands. Examples of such include the Oasis of Love, by Mrs Gloria Makongah; Rightway Bible Church, by Mrs Tina Adams; Church of God Mission, by Mrs Margaret Idahosa and Mrs Sarah Omaku of Family Worship Centre Abuja. Women see Pentecostalism as a way of liberation for women and a way which brings the gospel of Jesus' "liberation and proclamation of freedom for the prisoners and release to the oppressed," as relevant and apt to their situation (see Luke 4:18).

12. Pentecostalism as political agenda for Nigeria's leadership crisis. Marshall has linked Pentecostal growth in Nigeria to "post-colonial crises of government versus the born-again ethics and the spirits of the political economy" (13-14). For her, Pentecostal growth is strategic. "It is a raising of an army to combat political, economic and social systems" (Marshall, 13-14). It is also a response to combat the rising tide of radical Islamism, which became a major feature in Nigeria in the aftermath of the Iranian revolution in 1979. It also coincided with the global rise of religious fundamentalism. The wind of the revolution reverberated in some universities in northern Nigeria and left a legacy of Christian-Muslim clashes. It also radicalized Christian-Muslim relations on campuses, as was witnessed in Ahmadu Bello University, Zaria and Bayero University, Kano, among others. Marshall elaborates this point further:

> Winning Nigeria for Jesus means the projection into collective, public space of a highly political agenda. The image of the invading army sweeping all unbelievers in its path, expresses the political ambition of replacing a corrupt regime, a new form of righteous authority that presents itself as a unique path to individual and collective salvation (13-16).

The link of Pentecostal growth in Nigeria to political Christian activism is becoming popular in scholarly discourse.

13. The search for the charismatic and the miraculous. One of the enduring factors, that is still relevant in attracting members into Pentecostalism is the search for healing miracles and the display of miraculous signs and charismatic endowments. The ability to exhibit power encounters, deliverances and the power of "casting and binding" the evil forces, is still a major attraction to Pentecostalism. Today, new terms such as "anointing," "break through" and reference to God's call have emerged within this context. Pentecostal leaders are now gauged, by their perceived possession of such powers and these have become driving factors for their churches. This supports the point we had raised above, which leads people away from mainline churches.

14. Media Attraction. Pentecostalism has attracted a large membership from its unprecedented use of the media in all forms (radio, television and print). The liberalization of the media in the 1990s by the government was an added advantage to Pentecostalism when religious messages and advertisements were commercially broadcast. Taking their examples from the foreign media used by Christian Broadcasting Network (CBN), Trinity Broadcasting Network (TBN) and 700 Club, some Pentecostal churches in Nigeria today broadcast their programs on national and private media. Examples include, the "Atmosphere of Miracles" of Pastor Chris Oyakhilome airs television programs in most cities in Nigeria (and produces

millions of copies of daily devotionals (The Rhapsody of Realities) and CDs), T.B Joshua's Synagogue of All Nations Television Channel, Dunamis Television, and others who are planning to establish their own television channels. The strategic importance of this medium has brought many people to Pentecostalism. Through media resources it is easy to buy video and cassette tapes of messages, church magazines and newsletters. The new trend of cyber-evangelism might add yet another boost to Pentecostalism's spread.

15. The quest for the Holy Spirit experience. One of the major attractions towards Pentecostalism is the quest for the indwelling of the Holy Spirit reminiscent of the experience of the early apostles on Pentecost day (Acts, 2). The quest for charismatic experience, such as speaking in tongues, prophecy, healing, signs and wonders, and workings of the Holy Spirit, also, characterize the Pentecostal phenomenon and needs to be studied as well. The "born again" mark of regeneration and new ethics is seen as a fulfillment of the Old Testament prophecy of Joel 2:28, that needs to be shared within Pentecostalism. In fact, the role of the Holy Spirit who enabled the early apostles to exhibit the love, care, sharing and fellowship that the Pentecostals seek to re-enact, has drawn people to its fold. The thirst for the Holy Spirit experience is what Cox calls the discovery of the "primal spirituality" (103). The frenzy towards revival or re-awakening is

dependent on the key belief of the demonstration of power unleashed by the Holy Spirit.

16. Pentecostal closeness to African Traditional Spirituality. Pentecostalism has been seen to be close to African traditional religious worldviews. Scholars have found and connected Pentecostalism to African traditional religious worldviews, in terms of concepts of power and power consciousness, fear, the supernatural and holistic worldview, mystical forces, healing, prayer, ecstatic praise, worship and ritual (Anyanwu, 106). Thus, what the Pentecostals seem to emphasize are elements that had been de-emphasized in the older missionary Christianity, but that are being re-discovered for greater spirituality and meaning. For Anyanwu, Pentecostalism is the contextualization and Africanization of Christianity in Africa - hence its massive appeal (104). Thus, it could be asserted that Pentecostalism is fast growing due to its contextual efforts and adaptation. Richard Flory and Kimon H. Sargeant pointed out this fact when they wrote that, "Pentecostalism is vibrant, growing, and adapting to different social and cultural environment across the globe" (Flory and Kimon, 297).

From our discussion so far, certain challenges have arisen that need further probing and deeper attention:

i.   Apart from a few cases, Pentecostalism, through its social ministries and programs of national and spiritual awakening and transformation, has not been fully recognized and commended by the government.

ii. There is the need for an objective research into Pentecostalism, generally, in order to appreciate its contribution to Nigerian Christianity, to Africa, and to the world at large.

iii. Pentecostalism needs to recognize the mandate of the church to mission and the force of Islam, which are keys to the future of Christianity in Nigeria.

iv. Pentecostalism needs to activate its political force, in order to impact the nation's leadership crisis, and the challenge of good governance.

v. Pentecostalism in Nigeria has the challenge of championing the re-orientation, or re-discovery of ethical Christian values that will help to transform Nigeria. Such values include honesty, justice, integrity, accountability, humility, selfless service, hard work, love, compassion and acts of mercy. It can set the agenda for this process, by taking advantage of its massive followership.

Conclusion

The rise and growth of Pentecostalism in Nigeria, has recorded remarkable heights that need to be contextualized within Nigeria's socio-political and economic realities. Nigerian Pentecostalism has emerged as a major player in shaping global Christianity that cannot be ignored. It has the potential to shape Pentecostal theology, by determining its shape, direction and sustenance. The challenge for Pentecostalism in Nigeria, involves its ability to chart a transformative role in African Christianity. Pentecostal emphasis must develop a Pentecostal theology that is centered on the Biblical witness empowered by the Holy Spirit, the witness of the Pentecost age. The attraction and growth of Pentecostalism will continue, as Pentecostal Churches fulfill this role in leading a spiritual revolution that will impact individual and public lives of Nigerians.

CHAPTER 5

PENTECOSTALISM AND THE CHALLENGE OF HERMENEUTICS AND APPLICATION IN NIGERIA

Introduction

Christianity in Nigeria has witnessed some vibrancy in the last four decades with the rise and growth of Pentecostalism. Pentecostalism has provided "a contextualized Christianity in Africa" (Anderson, 122) and has the potential of shaping world Christianity. Anderson has particularly noted the "ability of African Pentecostalism to adapt to and fulfill religious aspiration that continues to be its main strength" (122). Nigeria could be described as the major hub of Pentecostal forces in Africa.

While Pentecostal waves in Nigeria have gone trans-national with influences around the world, Pentecostalism in Nigeria has not attracted much serious hermeneutical engagement. In general, Pentecostal theology has not been systematized or fully documented. What presently exists are a few published books, written by some Pentecostal leaders and lay members, which do not address the Biblical bases for Pentecostal beliefs, teachings and practices. Some other sources exist in church bulletins, booklets, Bible study guides and journals, but such cannot sustain Pentecostal theological reflections. The ever-growing "popular theology" which is propagated by the members within Pentecostalism, indicates the level of their Biblical understanding and application. Even the few existing materials on Pentecostalism in Nigeria, have not concentrated on the Pentecostal theological bases for their beliefs and practices. This problem becomes yet more acute when most writers on Pentecostalism in Nigeria are non-Pentecostals, whose writings are viewed by Pentecostals with a lot of suspicion and lack of trust. Examples of such writers include, Ogbu Kalu, Matthews A. Ojo, Musa B. Gaiya, Donatus Pius Ukpong, Deji Ayegboyin, Moses Olatunde Oladeji, O.B.E Josiah Amata, among others. Keith Warrington, quoting Clark observes that, "Pentecostal theology is researched at the researcher's peril" (17). Ojo situates this problem succinctly this way:

> Charismatics generally have not systematized their teachings, because they view theology with suspicion, even at times considering it as Satan's tool to mislead Christians. The teachings are many and diverse, and they are constantly stated and reformulated to keep the organizations in focus in establishing them... Charismatics' doctrinal emphases are noted in the literal interpretation of Bible verses; hence, they are intensely Biblical (20).

Warrington has shown that "early Pentecostals were suspicious of creeds and preferred to concentrate on shared experience" (20). He states that,

> That which is central to their faith and practice are
> the concepts of 'encounter' and 'experience.' They
> aim to know God experientially, whether it is via an
> intellectual recognition of his being or an emotional
> appreciation of his character and it is that often makes
> them functionally different from the Christian tradition
> (Warrington, 20).

In fact it is concluded from this that, "the essence of
Pentecostalism can hardly be captured by any theological
formulation; spirituality and spiritual experience is primary."
Pentecostal revelation

> . . . is not intended to affect the mind but also
> the emotions. Theology is not explored best in a
> rationalistic context alone but also with a readiness
> to encounter the divine and be impacted by one's
> discoveries in a way that will enlighten the mind but
> also to transform life.

Gyadu has supported Warrington, by noting that Pentecostals
theologize too, but prefers to speak of Pentecostal beliefs and
practices than of Pentecostal theology of the typical western
pedagogical type (Gyadu, 7). For Gyadu:

> The articulation of such beliefs and practices within
> Ghanaian Pentecostalism is based on members'
> experiences of the Spirit in which Pentecostals express
> or live out their faith. It encapsulates the cluster of
> values, beliefs and practices that give Pentecostals their
> distinctive Christianity (7).

Kalu sees Pentecostalism, as "a religious movement, a genre
of Christianity that should be understood both by what it says
and does" (249). He notes that, while they are defined by

their anti-intellectualism, Pentecostals rebut the oral theology that Jesus practiced and reject philosophical theology and the gymnastics of high and low critical methods (Kalu, 249). Anderson has further provided a close perspective about Pentecostal theology this way:

> To understand Pentecostal theology properly we also need to understand how Pentecostals and Charismatics read the Bible, which they acknowledge universally as the source of their theology. For most Pentecostals and Charismatics, theology is inseparable from the Bible in which they find their central message. Although identifying to a great extent with the evangelical position on Biblical authority, most Pentecostals are not usually preoccupied with polemical issues like the unity and inspiration of the Bible and other theological niceties. Their purpose in reading the Bible is to find something that can be experienced as relevant to their felt needs (225).

For the Pentecostals, it is the Holy Spirit who makes the Bible alive rather than "esoteric and theoretical principles" (Anderson, 226). Anderson indicates that, "early Pentecostals believed, following Paul, that God had called the weak and foolish things of this world to confound the wise" (261).

This chapter is hinged on certain presuppositions namely:

i.   Pentecostal theology has not been fully developed in Nigeria;

ii.   The type of Pentecostal theology that develops in Nigeria has the potential of shaping African Christianity to a great extent;

iii. Pentecostalism in Nigeria is incapable, at the moment, of developing Pentecostal theology that is also Biblical due to a lack of theologically trained minds that could engage in such an exercise;

iv. The multiplicity of Pentecostals with their distinctive emphases creates the problem of a lack of uniformity in their theological formulation;

v. A new hermeneutical paradigm and challenge has emerged from Pentecostal teaching and practice in Nigeria, which is being influenced by popular theology.

The chapter attempts to stimulate the hermeneutical challenges, which call for Pentecostal hermeneutical engagement in order to safeguard "inappropriate" application of Biblical message and witness.

Hermeneutics refers to the "science and art of Biblical interpretation" that requires a systematic procedure and skill in its handling (Virkler, 16). Biblical interpretation needs clear understanding. Nehemiah 8:8 says, "they read from the book of the law of God, making it clear and giving the meaning so that the people could understand what was being read."

Interpretation also requires correct handling, before it can be properly applied in daily life. In 2 Timothy 2:15, Paul instructed Timothy, by saying "Do your best to present yourself to God as one approved, a workman who does not need to be ashamed and who correctly handles the word of truth."

Application refers to the ability to relate Biblical teaching and its meaning to real life situations. It is making sense of the Biblical passage and it is also practical. It involves appropriation of such Biblical truths to life. Jesus himself said that one "who hears God's word and puts it into practice is like a wise man who built his house on the rock," but any one "who hears these words of mine and does not put them into practice is like a foolish man who built his house on the sand" (Matt 7:24, 26).

Jesus criticized the Jews for misinterpretation and incorrect application of the Scripture. Jesus asked his disciples and his hearers: "Have you not read?" (see Matt.12:3,5, Mk. 2:25; Lk.6:3) to draw their attention to the challenges of scriptural application.

Doriani has stated that "Biblical application promotes a relationship with God and conformity to him" (14). Doriani sees the principle of application pervading the entire scriptures as "interpretation and application coalesce and propel each other forward" (20). Similarly, Doriani quotes John Frame who observed rightly, "the meaning of scripture is its application" as "we understand scripture only when we know how to use it" (20). Doriani defines theology as, "the application of the word of God by persons to all areas of life," to meet spiritual needs and to promote godliness and spiritual health (20). However, Stenhall has cautioned that, sound "application cannot occur without correct exegesis." Making reference to 2 Tim. 3:16-17, Doriani speaks of Paul engaging in the theology of application and concludes that: "we need a theology of application, explaining how all scripture equips the Church for every good work" (Doriani, 41).

The Pharisees misread Moses and the prophets, and were incapable of applying the law correctly. Eventually, they became legalistic and evolved "traditions of men" which made them spiritually blind, though they remained externally religious without the transforming power of God.

As noted by Anderson and other scholars on Pentecostalism in Africa, Pentecostalism is contextual (250). It has been able to witness rapid growth, because of its ability to relate to the practical existential realities of life. The same is true with Pentecostalism in Nigeria. Ukpong states: "the basic characteristic of the contextual approach is its explicit engagement of the Biblical text with a specific context as a starting point and the acknowledgement of the contextual nature of the reading" (24).

This chapter focuses on a few sampled Pentecostal themes for further discussion. They include miracles, prayers and prosperity. The essence is to illustrate what could be termed "faces of Pentecostal theology" in Nigeria.

It is our conviction that theology is shaped and developed from community (peoples') experiences in faith, before taking a formal, systematized and codified form. This was also true of the early Christian community. The shift today in emphases within Nigerian Pentecostalism to some aspects such as prosperity, use of TV, and outward appearance in terms of dressing and dress patterns are marks of new hermeneutical reflections and application among others, that have become pertinent and imperative.

Some Pentecostal Beliefs and Practices in Nigeria

a. **Miracles:** Part of the Pentecostal mark is its emphasis on the "miraculous signs and wonders." Warrington writes, "this emphasis on divine healing is noticeable in Pentecostalism throughout the world, support resting on OT and NT texts, reinforced by occurrences of healing throughout its history" (267). He notes further that, "there has been in recent years an increasing readiness to develop a theology of healing by some Pentecostals that is analytical and critical of excess and errors" (Warrington, 267). Mark 16:14-20 says, "then the disciples went out and preached everywhere, and the Lord worked with them and confirmed his word by signs that accompanied it."

Philip Jenkins sees this verse as the "charter or foundation text of African missionary practice" (40). Ojo has also rightly observed that, "healings and miracles are central to and one of the illuminating expressions of the religious idea of Nigerian charismatics" (201). Ojo, however, provides a distinction between healings among non-Pentecostals and of the Pentecostal churches, and indicates that charismatics have evolved a term of "deliverance" which addresses the socio-political situation and economic problems of a country. Healing from all forms of difficulties and failures of life is termed "success and prosperity"

(Ojo, 201). It is Ojo's assertion that "Charismatics have appropriated their traditional African cultural backgrounds and have defined healing to include freedom from demonic attacks and oppression" (202). Warrington writes that the "belief that Jesus delegated his healing authority to all believers permeates Pentecostalism, though it also predates it" (282) and sees "the relationship between healing and evangelism as always being prominent in Pentecostalism" (Warrington, 281).

Other verses have also motivated Pentecostal belief. For example, Matthew 10:1 says, "Jesus called his twelve disciples to him and gave them authority to drive out spirits and to heal every diseases and sickness" (NIV).

John 16-23 says, "In that day you will no longer ask me anything, very truly I tell you, my father will give you whatever you ask in my name" (NIV).

The Pentecostals believe that they have authority "in the name of Jesus" to heal, cast out demons and to deliver those that are afflicted. This belief and motivation has attracted remarkable followership to Pentecostalism in Nigeria.

Acts 19:11 says: "God did extraordinary miracles through Paul, so that even handkerchiefs and aprons that had touched him were taken to the sick, and their illnesses were cured and evil spirits left them" (NIV).

This passage today has become very popular among Pentecostals in Nigeria, who use handkerchiefs for healing. They are advertised and sold, and have imputed the quality of "anointing" to whoever use them. Ayegboyin has noticed this trend among Pentecostals when he states that, "apart from the 'give and prosper messages' in some of these ministries, there is full-scale commercialization of the gospel through the sale of 'breakthrough handkerchiefs' (called 'mantles'), prayer books and vow making" (78). Storms had cautioned its use and abuse today, when he wrote that:

> Undoubtedly, many are uneasy with the passage in Acts because of outlandish attempts by certain faith healers to repeat the practice in our day. Often, unlike Paul, they charge a substantial fee for their clothes and anointed aprons (86).

The point of its abuse, by commercialization and imputing interpretation and application beyond the context of the verse, depicts the level of the hermeneutical flaw and wrong application that Pentecostals have developed in Nigeria. The idea of spiritual anointing flowing, or transferring, by using handkerchiefs is strange to the passage, but has gained currency among those who have also popularized "feet washing." Feet washing services have gained prominence, as occasions to receive anointing, and the water used in such rituals is, often times, preserved and used as people believe that it attracts prosperity, favour and blessing. Some of such "feet washing" services have attracted large crowds, without taking a second look at the understanding of Jesus' act in the context, which was meant to teach humility and service (see Jn. 13:15). Because of the quest for power, anointing has become a major catch phrase for the search for God's hand and touch on people's lives, which some Pentecostals believe is a gateway towards performing miracles and a mark of God's seal on them.

Warrington has also noted that anointing with oil, has retained its place in the context of prayer for the sick in Pentecostal practice (Jas 5:6), though it is not viewed as being essential for healing to occur (291). He also identifies that some African Pentecostals use anointing oil in settings where curses are removed, or reversals in life situations are requested, or in the impartation of power for those who are to undertake specific responsibilities in the church (Warrington, 291). Warrington traces the use of anointing oil, associated with presence of the Spirit from its use in covenant rituals, and association with the bestowal of honor and affirmation (293). He sees this as a significant feature of Pentecostal healing practice. Ajibade has provided details of this practice among Pentecostals in Nigeria this way:

> One popular charismatic practice today is "anointing the sick with oil." The practice is so much cherished that some ministers do not get out of their homes without a bottle of olive oil in their pockets. Church members too have made "olive oil" a constant

> companion as one can see a bottle in their
> bags, cars, offices, shops and open places in
> their homes. Anointing services are popular
> programs that attract mass attendance and
> testimonies of healing and other miracles are
> shared from time to time in such gatherings
> (166).

When anointing powers are sought after, with all the imputations of interpretation and application of Biblical texts to their beliefs and practices, the results of these are what we presently witness as outlined by Ajibade above.

b. **Prayer:** Ayegboyin has asserted that, "the universal and frequent facet of the new Pentecostal Churches (NPCs) spirituality as well as worship is their intense stress on prayer" (75). In other words, prayer is a major mark of Pentecostals. Prayer was a distinctive feature of early African Independent Churches (AICs), out of which their name "Aladura," "praying churches" emerged. John S. Mbiti had noted that, "prayers, more than any other aspect of religion, contain the most intense expression of African traditional spirituality" (70).

Ayegboyin has provided a characterisation of such prayers among Pentecostals writing:

> In most NPCs, prayers are contextualized
> to match with prayers, which the Africans
> used to pray in the traditional society. The
> NPCs pray out loud, individually and with
> enthusiasm repeating some catch phrases

> like, in the name of Jesus, Holy Spirit, blood
> of Jesus, and Holy Ghost fire among others.
> They memorize and recite some verses or
> portions of scriptures when praying. This is
> described as conceiving the word in the heart
> (75).

Popular verses used by Pentecostals include, Isaiah 54:17, "No weapon forged against you will prevail, and you will refute every tongue that accuses you" (NIV).

This is a popular and often quoted, verse, that is used also in spiritual warfare prayers. A closely related verse to this is Mark 7:8, that says, "Do not gloat over me, my enemy, though I have fallen, I will arise, though I sit in darkness the Lord is my light" (NIV).

Others include, Luke 11:1, which says, "One day Jesus was praying in a certain place. When he had finished one of his disciples said to him, Lord, teach us to pray just as John taught his disciples" (NIV).

Mark 1:35 says, "Very early in the morning, while it was still dark, Jesus got up, left the house and went off to a solitary place, where he prayed" (NIV).

Mark 6:46 says, "After leaving them, he went up on a mountain side to pray" (see also Lk. 5:16; Lk. 11:1) (NIV).

Pentecostals emphasise prayers, fasting, night vigils and personal commitment to prayer life as Warrington rightly notes, "prayer has been recognised as an opportunity not only for requesting but also for listening to divine advice and guidance as to how one should pray in contexts of sickness as well as other settings" (Warrington, 287-288). Such "other settings" include spiritual warfare prayers and praying down the Holy Ghost Fire to consume enemies and forces of darkness that hinder one's growth and progress. It is within such a context that the spiritual warfare prayers of the Mountain of Fire and Miracle Ministries (MFM) can be understood.

Mountain of Fire and Miracle Ministries is one of the largest and fastest growing Christian congregations in Africa (Ayegboyin, 37). The ministry is particularly noticeable because of its use of imprecatory and curse prayers that Adogame classifies as the "security gospel."

Dr. D.K. Olukoya is the Pastor and General Overseer of the Mountain of Fire and Miracles Ministries. He has written books on spiritual warfare providing strategies to confront evil powers. Some of such titles of his books include, *Prayer Warfare Against 70 Mad Spirits, Wasting the Wasters, Overcoming Witchcraft,* and *Power Against Destiny Quenchers,* among others. "Prayer points" are provided for each prayer, depending on the nature of the problem being addressed.

Mountain of Fire and Miracle Ministries has been considered as a training ground where people are taught how to, individually, face life challenges and problems with the spiritual weapons of warfare including,

> Praying 'militantly,' with bullets of fire and thunder, slaying enemy with 'arrows of fire' and 'swords of deliverance,' paralyzing the adversary by binding the 'strongman' and bulldozing his stronghold, terminating the operations of satanic powers by destroying spiritual padlocks and destroying the gates of Beelzebub (Ayegboyin, 37).

Pentecostals in Nigeria literally interpret and apply Ephesians 6:12. It says,

> For our struggle is not against flesh and blood, but against the rulers, against the authorities, against the powers of this dark world and against the spiritual forces of evil in heavenly realms.

The use of biblical metaphors and symbolism has been popularised in Pentecostal vocabulary, particularly among MFM members and those who are engaged in spiritual warfare. Such language and tone are also reflected in the lyrics of some Pentecostal singers, such as Broda Martin in Lagos who sees Jesus as the "bulldozer" against enemies; and in Princess Oluchi Okeke of Wonders of Praise Ministry, Onitsha. For example, in Princess Oluchi Okeke's song in *Battle Praise* Vol. 2, she renders thus:

Preamble
Oh God of vengeance (2x)
The mighty man of battle,

the chief corner stone,
The I am that I am... (Igbo lyrics
of exaltation of God)
Response by all
Lyrics continue
Arise oh Lord and let your enemies be scattered...
(speaks in tongues...).
Fight my battle (2x)
Holy Ghost arise and fight my battle (2x)
Arise today Holy Ghost and fight my battle. Enough
is enough (2x)
Holy Ghost arise and fight my battle... Halleluyah...
The Lord is fighting your battle right now...
Evil arrow, go back to your sender (2x)
Arrow of poverty go back to your sender (2x)
Arrow of shame go back to your sender (2x)
Occultic arrow go back to your sender (2x)
Every arrow is returning back now in the name of
Jesus
I command them to come out now
Blood of Jesus (2x) fight my battle (2x).
The Bible says, "we overcome them by the blood of
the lamb"... Jesus is fighting for you now.
Any power standing on my way fall down and die
(2x)
any wizard, witches standing on my way fall down
and die fall down and die... owners of evil load carry
your load (2x)
Owners of my problem, carry your load (2x)
Owners of my sorrow/trouble carry your load (2x)

Holy Ghost show them pepper
Holy Ghost show them fire
Holy Ghost show them thunder
Blood of Jesus pursue them...

The song is performed, with much dance and energy, in a battle-ready posture of confronting the evil one and dismantling his powers.

Appraising MFM's "theology of deliverance," Ayegboyin has raised some pertinent questions and observations:

i.   Is it not possible that witches, wizards and forces of evil have been elevated so much and are possible figments of the imagination?

ii. More ground is being conceded to demons than the gospels permit;

iii. African Christians have manufactured demons and enlarged their space in theology; and

iv. The "MFM's vocabulary and methodology in prayer rites are bizarre" (Ayegboyin, 58).

Ayegboyin believes that although the MFM use verses from Isaiah 54:17 and Micah 7:8, their pronouncements such as: "let my enemy die, die now in Jesus' name," or "let those who seek my downfall roast in hell," are offensive to the Gospel on the grounds that they pervert the evangelical message (58).

However, Pastor Olukoya, the General Overseer of the MFM, has countered Ayegboyin. He maintains that the "demonological theology" of the MFM is grounded in Christian experience and conforms to New Testament teaching. Thus the MFM is one of the churches that is out to exorcise Africa from its demonic powers in order to liberate her from the thraldom of the "prince of the air" (Ayegboyin, 58). Ayegboyin concludes that the "MFM is speaking the language that the people understand" (59). However, it must conform to Biblical understanding, because, as he later accepts, there is a growing concern about Deliverance Ministries and of the NPCs in respect of "their contempt for theological erudition, or, generally, their disregard for sound teaching of the word."

David T. Adamo has also studied some aspects of the prayers that have been popularized and used within Pentecostal circles. These include imprecatory, therapeutic, and protective prayer, plus curses, and prayers to invoke death. He sees this as close to African traditional religion (Adamo 18). He shows how specific Psalms are used for protection like Psalm 5, 6, 28, 35, 37, 54, 55, 83, and 109. Others include Psalms to invoke death (Ps 55:15, 23) and to drive out evil plans (Ps. 35). For example, Psalm 5:4-6,10 read thus,

> For you are not a God who is pleased with wickedness; with you evil people are not welcome. The arrogant cannot stand in your

> presence. You hate all who do wrong; you destroy those who tell lies. The blood thirsty and deceitful you, Lord detest... Declare them guilty, O God! Let their intrigues be their downfall. Banish them for their many sins, for they have rebelled against you.

Psalm 55:15 says, "Let death take them by surprise; let them go down alive to the realm of the dead, for evil friends lodging among them."

"But you, God, will bring down the wicked into the pit of decay; the blood thirsty and deceitful will not live out half their days" (Ps. 55:23) (NIV).

For Ademiluka, "the African reader understands the enemies of the Psalmist as none other than witches, sorcerers and all those who have hatred for him" (58).

Other popular Pentecostal verses include Isaiah 49:25 which says, "But this is what the Lord says; yes, captives will be taken from warriors, and plunder retrieved from the fierce; I will contend with those who contend with you, and your children I will save" (NIV).

Joel 2:25 says, "I will repay you for the years the locusts have eaten - the great locust and the young locust, the other locusts and the locust swarm - my great army that I sent among you" (NIV).

Missionary Christianity did not emphasize spiritual warfare. As a result, there are Christians throughout Africa, who could not provide answers to the crippling cases of evil, demon possession, witchcraft, sorcery, and so on. The Bible was presented as incapable of providing answers to these supernatural forces. This explains why Pentecostal concepts of spiritual warfare and the strategies needed for such, are not only a rediscovery of this Biblical reality, but an agenda which seeks to confront and engage the forces of this world (demonic) with the Gospel in order to establish God's reign here on earth. It can therefore be argued that Pentecostal attempts to experience the benefits of God's presence is part and parcel of their understanding of "realized eschatology."

c. **Prosperity.** The Pentecostal emphasis on prosperity and blessing in order to attract "the good things of life," has attracted considerable public comment, reaction and scrutiny. It is also in this area that Pentecostal hermeneutical engagement and application has been challenged. Not that this emphasis remains unchanged, as there seems to have been a shift from the 1970s era prosperity theology of Archbishop Benson Idahosa, the "pastor who brought the prosperity and faith gospel to Nigeria" (Marshall 181). Instead, there is an increasing emphasis on economic empowerment, leadership training and a focus on the poor and the dispossessed. These themes are preached by such as Pastor Sam Adeyemi, David Oyedepo, Chris Oyakhilome and Pastor Enoch Adeboye. Prosperity gospel preachers take Jesus' words literally, when he said, "the thief comes only to steal and kill and destroy; I have come that they may have life and have it to the full" (Jn. 10:10). Prosperity preachers use Biblical verses to solicit for members' support for church work, or to explain their own personal commitment to the pursuit of a good life. For example, 1 Corinthians 9:7-14 is quoted to justify eating from the labour of preaching the Gospel. Verse 14 of the same passage says, "In the same way, the Lord has commanded that those who preach the gospel receive their living from the gospel." Its closely related verse is 1 Timothy 5:18, which says: "Do not muzzle the ox while it is treading out the grain, and the worker deserves his wages."

Pentecostals have also attempted to "correct" what they perceive as "wrong teaching" arising from an interpretation of 1 Timothy 6:10 which says, "For the love of money is a root of all kinds of evil. Some people eager for money and have wandered from the faith and pierced themselves with griefs." In the attempt, by Pentecostals, to "correct" this wrong application, where missionaries de-emphasized acquisition and quest for wealth, Pastor Sam Adeyemi sees the emergence today of what he calls "twisted theology."

An area, that the Pentecostals have brought to the fore, in their interpretation and application of Biblical passages, is giving. Taking Luke 6:38 literally, they have provided several interpretations. The verse says:

> Give, and it will be given to you. A good
> measure, pressed down, shaken together and

> running over, will be poured into your lap.
> For with the measure you use, it will be
> measured to you (NIV).

To say that Pentecostals have mastered the art of giving, in order to attract God's blessing is not an exaggeration. Giving of alms is called different names, such as offering and seed money or sowing. Ayegboyin writes on this as follows:

> The new Pentecostal churches emphasize
> the seed faith principles of sowing and
> reaping. The preachers have various ways of
> persuading people to give. They admonish
> their adherents to give a variety of
> offerings – seed offerings, covenant offering,
> breakthrough offerings, success offerings and
> the like (78).

Closely related to Luke 6:38 is Jesus' promise to his disciples in Mark 10:29-30:

> I will tell you the truth, no one who has
> left home or brothers or sisters or mother or
> father or children or fields for me and the
> gospel will fail to receive a hundred times as
> much in this present age (homes, brothers,
> sisters, mothers, children and fields-and with
> them, persecutions) and in the age to come,
> eternal life (NIV).

John 16:23 has also attracted Pentecostal usage. It says, "In that day, you will no longer ask me anything. I tell you the truth, my Father will give you whatever you ask in my name" (NIV).

This verse is set in close association with Jesus' words in Matthew 7:7:

> Ask and it will be given to you; seek and you will find; knock and the door will be opened to you. For everyone who asks receives, he who seeks finds; and to him who knocks, the door will be opened.

Haggai 2:8 has also attracted Pentecostal use and application in their emphasis and teaching. The verse says, "the silver is mine and the gold is mine, declares the Lord Almighty. The glory of this present house will be greater than the glory of the former, says the Lord Almighty." Even Genesis 2:11, which mentions the "entire land of Havilah, where there is gold," has found some allusions among Pentecostals who draw application from it. Some Pentecostals have given their businesses symbolic names such as, "Havilah Restaurant," "Havilah Bakery," and so on.

When Pentecostals put such verses together, they easily provide an interpretation to justify their emphasis on the "name it and claim it" theology that is fundamental to prosperity teaching.

Thus, some see Pentecostal teaching and application in its literal sense, as wrong hermeneutics since it has provided a Christianity that is devoid of hunger, suffering and death. This popular Pentecostal chorus caps it all:

Me I no go suffer,
I no go beg for bread (2x),

God of miracle na my papa oh! (2x).
Literally translated as:
I will not suffer
I will not beg for bread (2x)
God of miracle is my father oh! (2x).

It can, therefore, be argued that the interpretation of such verses explains the lifestyle of some Pentecostals. For example, Ruth Marshall has discussed Pentecostal prosperity beliefs and practices, when she refers to Bishop Idahosa's wealthy legacy through the creation of an empire including:

> The miracle centre, stadium, a hospital, a private university, luxury guest residences and a bank . . . The family owns a huge shopping complex and luxury villas in Nigeria, London, and the United States, as well as a fleet of luxury cars (Marshall, 178-79).

She notes that,

> The advent of the doctrine of prosperity and the Word-Faith Movement provided the discursive and symbolic platform on which to integrate the Born Again experience of redemption with social mobility, conspicuous consumption, and the legitimation of wealth in a time of scarcity (180).

Using scriptural citations to acquire wealth, Marshall refers to Pastor Kris Okotie of the House of God

Church, who bought a new BMW automobile in 1992 for his wife and quoted James 1:17, "every good gift and every perfect gift is from above, and cometh down from the Father of lights" (Marshall, 181).

Stories of other Pentecostal leaders, such as Pastor Chris Oyakhilome, Pastor Enoch Adeboye, and Pastor David Oyedepo, have attracted media reportage in Nigeria. Captions include such titles as, "Church Empires: Their Billions, Their Assets, their Scandals;" "The Miracle Workers: New Generation Pastors Turn Churches Into Money Making Ventures;" "Pastors of Thieves: How Oyakilome Received Another Stolen Money," and "Nigeria's Richest Pastors: Their Businesses and Infuences." These stories revealed their various sources and use of wealth, including money raised from sales of tapes and CDs, gifts, educational institutions such as universities, and other investments.

The resultant effects of such teaching on prosperity is that Pentecostals display this ostentatious, profligate and flamboyant lifestyle in the conviction that they are showing off God's visitation and the anointing they have received.

A verse that has received Pentecostal attention, in respect of giving of alms is Malachi 3:8:

> Will a man rob God? Yet you rob me. But you ask, 'How do we rob you?' In tithes and offerings. You are under a curse – the whole nation of you – because you are robbing me. Bring the whole tithe into the storehouse,

that there may be food in my house. "Test me
in this," says the Lord Almighty and see if I
will not throw open the floodgates of heaven
and pour out so much blessing that you will
not have room enough for it (NIV).

For Pentecostals, "tithing is not only leading to the
experience of prosperity but it is also a passport to
heaven" (Ukpong (a), 130). Ukpong (a) has referred
to the Redeemed Christian Church of God (RCCG)
and other Pentecostal churches, who believe that
"regular payment of tithe and offering is obligatory
because it is God's command" (129a). Blessing in
abundance is promised to those who faithfully pay
their tithes from their earnings, through salary,
inheritance, gifts, business profits, transactions and
interests from bank accounts.

On tithes and offerings as "Malachi rhetoric" in
RCCG, Adogame has clarified significantly that:

While RCCG strongly encourages its members
to engage in tithing, members are not
compelled to do so. Still, the liturgical
structure makes ample space for the
collection of tithes. And within the sermons,
the off-cited Biblical references are cited
as a way of calling members to wake up
to their responsibility. It is believed that
unfaithfulness in the area of tithing can
make a member lose God's blessing, because
he is perceived as stealing directly from
God. The failure to pay tithes is believed to

> automatically bring a curse on a member and
> his or her business (198).

Adogame indicates further that:

> The enormous financial resources generated
> through tithing are primarily geared toward
> the welfare of ministers and church
> employees, as well as for the poor and the
> needy in the church. In spite of this, only a
> small percentage of RCCG pastors earn their
> pay from the church. Several local pastors
> operate as honorary pastors, while others
> are supported materially from local parishes
> (200).

However, as a result of the quest to attract God's blessing and prosperity through offerings and tithes, some members have used stolen money from their work place to offer to the church.

The story, which made headlines of this "scandal," was elaborately uncovered in the Christ Embassy Church (*The News*, 22-27). Reflecting on this, Ayegboyin stated:

> The new Pentecostals have produced their
> fair share of dangerous swindlers. It is well
> known in Nigeria that a number of prosperity
> preachers do not emphasize ethical practices
> in their teachings. Evidently, this group
> has produced its fair share of dangerous
> charlatans, frauds and extortionists, who ask
> for tithes from well known "drug pushers,"

> "armed bandits" and fake contractors (Ayegboyin, 84).

This is the danger when hermeneutics and application of Biblical verses are taken to the extreme, which could lead to misapplication and errors.

Pentecostals have been accused of proof texting, that is, "stringing together an inappropriate or inadequate series of Bible verses to prove thier theology" (Omenyo, 51-2). They also have been perceived to be involved in "selective theologizing," and "isolationism" that is, carefully and skillfully selecting passages that "speak to their situation." They are accused of failure to correctly interpret a single scripture text, because the immediate context is ignored, and "spiritualizing," namely, reading our meaning to the text (i.e. eisegesis) instead of exegesis (Mayhue, 89-95).

Hermeneutical Challenges

From the foregoing, we have identified some hermeneutical challenges that need to be addressed, by Pentecostals in Nigeria.

i. The need for sound Pentecostal theology. Some Pentecostal churches in Nigeria have an elite leadership. This is to say that some of the founders, leaders and Senior Pastors have at least a university degree. Indeed some have Ph.D degrees and were formerly university lecturers, such as Pastor Enoch

Adeboye of the Redeemed Christian Church of God (RCCG), and Pastor W.F. Kumuyi of the Deeper Life Bible Church. They can and are, therefore, capable of engaging in hermeneutics, in order to sharpen the Pentecostal hermeneutical engagement.

Omenyo has shown Pentecostals' need for theological education writing that Pentecostal schools that emerged from the 1980s, produced only *crude rationalism* with an emphasis on *oral theology* (51-52).

Although a few Pentecostal churches have set up their Bible schools, these schools lack depth, concentrating instead on leadership training. Omenyo throws out a challenge that,

> ...since the growth of Pentecostal churches in Africa is mainly due to the perception that they address particular African needs, something western missionaries have proved unable to do well, there is the need for African oriented theological education(Omenyo, 52).

When Pentecostals are able to train their clergy and those involved in church ministry well, Pentecostal theology can be developed as those involved would be equipped to handle hermeneutical areas adequately.

ii. Pentecostals' need for Biblical, contextual hermeneutics. One of the major contributions of Pentecostalism in Nigeria today, is contextualization efforts in its preaching, teaching and practice.

The Bible evolved within certain contexts, which shaped its message. Missionary Christianity *failed* to contextualize the Gospel message in Africa, hence its reverberation effects after its acceptance by Africans. As Pentecostals engage in contextualization efforts, it must be safeguarded against error or the temptation and trap of compromising Biblical message with African traditional cultural beliefs and practices. Instead, African traditional beliefs and practices should be enriched and transformed by the Gospel, leading to the emergence of an acceptable global Christianity. Pentecostals in Nigeria should be able to provide this significant prophetic role, in order to maintain the Holy Spirit filled encounter.

iii. The call for commitment to the hermeneutical task. The task of hermeneutics is tedious, difficult, and demands time, skill, commitment and dexterity. It calls for sincerity among Pentecostals, who typically prefer to go to the evangelization fields because the *souls are perishing,* or because *the harvest is plentiful and the labourers are few.* Instead of that, they should rather be getting better equipped, through the handling of the Word of truth (the Bible) which will yield a greater impact among people than what we presently witness. Pentecostals in Nigeria need to appreciate and accept this need, and pursue it as part of their shift in paradigm.

iv. The need to codify Pentecostal theology in Nigeria. As we have noted earlier, it is mostly non-Pentecostals who have written on Pentecostalism in Nigeria. Today, apart from Alan Isaacson's book on the Deeper Life published in 1990, and Matthew Ojo's book on *The End – Time Army. Charismatic Movements in Modern Nigeria* (2006), Asonzeh F.K. Ukah's Ph.D. on the RCCG, and a few others, books have not addressed specific Pentecostal theological positions. Both Pentecostal and non-Pentecostal scholars, therefore, need to engage with each other on these issues and so develop Pentecostal theological beliefs.

v. Monitoring Pentecostal theology in Nigeria. To be able to safeguard against popular but inappropriate teaching and practices among Pentecostals, some monitoring and control needs to be exercised. The Pentecostal Fellowship of Nigeria (PFN) can play this role, although it is noted that not all Pentecostal churches belong to the PFN. The Christian Association of Nigeria (CAN), which is a larger and broader umbrella body of Christians, can assist in this regard.

Conclusion

The reality of the outpouring of the Holy Spirit in this age has been partly evident, through the Pentecostal experience in Nigeria. The phenomenon of the stirring of the Holy Spirit is recorded in history across the ages. Since the last century, Nigeria has witnessed the Holy Spirit at work through early precursors such as Garrick Braide and founders of the African Independent Churches (AICs). As documented by many African scholars and outsiders alike, the break away from mainline missionary churches was a reaction to missionary Christianity then being preached.

It was to address this "missionary Christianity" that Pentecostalism emerged and has flourished with its contextualization efforts to relate the Gospel to the existential realities of daily life. In their efforts to apply the Bible, however, there have been observable hermeneutical challenges to their beliefs, emphases and practices. Sometimes, some Pentecostal beliefs and practices have resorted to African traditional religious worldviews that provides them grounds for drawing parallels in their application. Such engagement however, must safeguard against "popular theologizing" which lacks Biblical roots. Land has added his voice to this caution thus:

> But Pentecostals must see the connection between this passion for the kingdom and theology lest they lose both through neglect or dissipation. Theology itself is a kind of passion for God, and passion for God requires ongoing theological work as part of its inner logic and worldly vocation (219).

As Pentecostals proclaim life to the people, through the Gospel of Jesus Christ and in their practical theologizing, they need to reflect on some of their beliefs, emphases and practices, in order to remain relevant to the Pentecostal core values as identified by Cox when he states that:

> My conviction is that Pentecostals have touched so many people because they have indeed restored something. It has succeeded because it has spoken to the spiritual emptiness of our time by reaching beyond the levels of creeds and ceremony into the

> core of human religiousness, into what might be called
> "primary spirituality" (81).

According to Cox, Pentecostalism has enabled "countless people to recover, on quite a personal level, three dimensions of this elemental spirituality that I call 'primal speech, 'primary piety,' and 'primal hope'.76" As the Pentecostals are challenged about the need for hermeneutical engagement, the Pentecostal "alternative metaphors" of born again ethics and redemption should provide a new vision of Christian values in Nigeria, for the Godly transformation that we all yearn for.

CHAPTER 6

PENTECOSTALISM AND THE CHALLENGES "OF CHARLATANS AND MAGICIANS"

An Understanding of Acts 8:9-25 in the Light of Pentecostal Experience in Nigeria

Introduction

Africa has witnessed the unprecedented growth and expansion of Pentecostalism, in the last four decades. Nigeria has emerged as one of the countries in Africa with the fastest growth rate of Pentecostalism. The so-called global shift of Christianity to the South, has led to Nigeria assuming the undisputable lead of providing the direction of Christianity in Africa. Moreover, it cannot be overstated to say that Pentecostalism today, has become one of the most vibrant streams of Christianity in Nigeria. The phenomenal growth of Christianity in Nigeria is tied to the Pentecostal influence which is believed to be a new wave of the outpouring of the Holy Spirit. Writing on the Pentecostal experience, J. Kwabena Asamoah Gyadu says:

> Pentecostalism may be understood as that stream of
> Christianity, which emphasizes personal salvation in
> Christ as a transformative experience wrought by the
> Holy Spirit; and in which such pneumatic phenomena
> as 'speaking in tongues,' prophecies, visions, healing,
> miracles, and signs and wonders in general, are sought,
> accepted, valued and consciously encouraged among
> members as evidence of the active presence of God's
> Spirit (1).

Emerging patterns of Pentecostal expressions, emphases and
theologies, have called for attempts to look at Acts 8:9-25,
and seek to relate the passage to current Pentecostal practice
in Nigeria, with particular reflection on the "charlatans" and
"magicians," who have disguised themselves as workers of
God's miracles and as using God's powers. The charismatic
show of these gifts of the Holy Spirit is one of the attractions
behind Pentecostal influx and growth.

A re-reading of Acts 8:9-25, with specific reference to
"Simon the Sorcerer," calls for a new understanding and
applicability in regards to Pentecostal practice in Nigeria.
Some pertinent questions have arisen, namely: What can be
learnt from the story of Simon the sorcerer, when it comes
to the quest for power, and working of signs and wonders?
What is the role of the Holy Spirit in healing ministry? Can the
power to perform signs and wonders be sold or bought? Are
there charlatans and magicians today among some Pentecostal
preachers, who pose as God's agents of his outpouring and
outworking powers? These and other related puzzles are what
this chapter seeks to address.

The Setting of Acts 8:9-25

The Acts of the Apostles provides a history of the formation, growth and expansion of the early church. It also records the supernatural outworking of the Holy Spirit who provided the power and enablement for the apostolic exploits of the early church. In the words of William Barclay, "the Holy Spirit is on almost every page of Acts" (249).

The Acts of the Apostles has attracted recent and intense study, because of its relevance to the contemporary Christian experience of Pentecostal explosion and expression of the Holy Spirit around the world. Writing on the relevance of the Acts of the Apostles, Dennis E. Johnson says, "it is obvious that we need light from the church's early days to shine in our churches today. God still speaks in them, we can learn from them and apply them in this century" (2). This assertion is corroborated by Conrad Gempf thus:

> Acts is relevant for people in all situations and cultures in so far as it provides godly examples, and assurance that however things look, God is at work behind the scenes, as He has been with His people in the past (1068).

Gempt notes that Acts teaches us about our situations and ourselves by drawing on the examples of others in similar situations (1068). It is among the lessons arising from the "examples of other people," that this chapter is situated, particularly with the example of Simon the magician.

The Acts of the Apostles also records the redemptive history of God's acts in history, which culminated in the death and resurrection of Jesus. This prophetic witness, which was preached by the apostles, was the core of the *kerygma* of the early church. The salvific motifs that underlie most of the Acts passages portray God, as the master in the divine drama of man's salvation. All these benefits are attainable and achieved, within the framework of the Holy Spirit.

Acts 8:9-25 is chosen because it finds contemporary relevance and application. Today we are in an era where "charlatans and magicians" have disguised themselves as workers of miracles, of signs and wonders, under the pretext of experiencing a Holy Spirit encounter, plus we find counterfeit miracles in Christian ministry leading many astray. Because of the fervour for the miraculous, the "Simonic Spirit," namely of offering and attempting to buy God's power, seems to have infiltrated some Pentecostal practices. The passages are chosen, therefore, as Paul Mumo Kisau has noted, "with reference to Acts 8 the inclusiveness of the passage to the Samaritans has relevance to Africans" (164). Contextualizing the text within the Nigerian milieu, will provide significant insights and practical areas of application that will challenge modern Pentecostal practice.

Of Charlatans and Magicians

The passage under consideration has provided certain details about Simon the magician who encountered Philip. Acts 9-11 indicates, "Simon had practiced sorcery in the city and amazed all the people in Samaria." He also boasted that he was someone great, "and all the people, both high and low, gave him their attention and exclaimed him as the Great Power." He also attracted a great following, for he had amazed people with his magic for a long time.

Oxford Advanced Learners' Dictionary defines charlatan, "as a person who claims to have knowledge or skills that they do not really have" (Hornby, 227). In other words, a charlatan is fake and manipulative. *The Concise Edition Dictionary and Thesaurus* adds other attributes of a charlatan to include cheat, empiric, impostor, pretender and quack (411).

The word "charlatan" is used in this work to refer to performing signs and wonders that are not of God but depending on magical manipulative tactics. Keener has noted that, "signs were accorded high evidential value in antiquity" (344). He also says that, "magicians usually drew large followings in antiquity" (Keener, 344). They are addressed in many ways, as sorcerers, "worshippers of fire," and jugglers among Persians, Arabians, Hindu and Chinese. They are also referred to as diviners, enchanters, conjurors, magicians, or magico-charismatic exorcists.

The word "magic" is used six times in the Bible, three times in the Old Testament and three times in the New Testament. In addition, the word "magicians" is used fifteen times.

The Old Testament acknowledged the existence of magicians, though it did not approve of them. They are described in various ways as:

i.   Sorcerers – people who used charms and spells (Ex. 22:18; Deut. 18:10; Is. 47:9, 12; Jer. 27:9).

ii. Magicians – Egyptian chief lector-priests were popular (Ex. 7:11, 22) who and were engaged in "secret arts" (Acts 19:19).

iii. Enchanters and charmers (Deut. 18:11; Is. 49:9, 12). Deuteronomy 18:11 identifies them as also engaging in witchcraft. Daniel 2:2 mentions magicians along with enchanters, sorcerers and astrologers, who mastered in interpretation of dreams (see also Num. 23:23; 24:1).

iv. Diviners and false prophets (Ezek. 21:21; Jer. 14:14; Ezek. 13:6), who see false visions, engage in idolatries and the "delusions of their minds."

v. Experts in charms and snake charmers (Ps. 58:5; Eccl. 10:11; Jer. 18:17).

vi. Sinners who will be punished (Rev. 18:23; 22:15; Gal. 5:20).

There are other references to magicians. For example, Exodus 7:11 records magicians who copied (imitated) Moses in turning their rods into serpents and water into blood (Ex. 7:22); who produced frogs (8:7), but failed to produce lice (8:18-19) and were afflicted by the boils (Ex. 9:11).

Jezebel, the wife of King Ahab, practiced sorcery (2 Kings 9:22). Manasseh, King of Judah encouraged it (2 Kings 21:6), and "he did much evil in the eyes of the Lord, provoking him to anger." The prophets also condemned it (see Mic. 5:12).

In Egypt, the priestly elite attached to the temples practiced magic. The *asipu* priest, performed exorcisms by the virtue of the gods, *Ea* and *Marduk*, the master magicians. This was also condemned by other nations (Lev. 20:27; Deut. 18:10-14). Though later Judaism recognized pagan sorcerers who could do miracles, they were attributed to Belial (Satan) (Ex. 7:11; 8:7).

Johnson has attempted to provide an etymology of the Greek term "magus," which originally referred to a member of the priestly caste in Persia and later to possessors of supernatural knowledge and power. In the Hellenistic Roman world, "magic" focused on the manipulation of supernatural forces for the benefit of individuals (Johnson 168). Buttressing this point further, Twelftree captured magic in the early church era thus, "In the modern study of early Christianity, the view has been that exorcism played a significant role in the success of early Christianity" (Twelftree 26). For Ramsay Macmullen, not only were miracles the primary engine for producing conversions in the ancient world, but also exorcism was possibly the most highly rated activity of the early Christian church. From Justin, Tertullian, Cyprian and Eusebius, Twelftree concludes that, although the institution of exorcism had taproots in Judaism and was of little account otherwise, "in Christianity, it found an extraordinary flowering and was essential in its growth" (Twelftree, 27).

From the foregoing, therefore, magicians, sorcerers or exorcists had prominent roles in ancient Biblical times and were popular. They drew a large following, as was demonstrated in the Aesculapius' healing homes of the Greco-Roman world. It is within this context that the text of our study can be understood.

Acts 8:9 mentions that Simon practiced sorcery in the city amazing the people of Samaria. Samaria (Sebaste) was a Gentile region of mixed population. The country of Samaria was diseased, possessed and deluded. They were possessed with demons, unclean spirits and false ideas. Jewish animosity with Samaritans was well-known (Jn. 4:9). The Samaritans were largely Babylonians by race (2 Kings 17:24; Ezra 4:9-10). 2 Kings 17:41 shows that while the Samaritans worshipped the Lord, they also served their "gods." It was into this type of religious environment that Simon was born. This was the environment, in which he commenced his own "ministry" and was finally proclaimed, the "great one, the great power of God" (Acts 8:9-10). Luke indicates that Judean Jews viewed Samaritans at best as half-breeds and at worst foreigners.

It is within this period that Simon emerges in the text of our consideration here. For some time, Simon had practiced sorcery in the city and amazed the people of Samaria.

Simon had boasted that he was someone great and people followed him in large numbers acclaiming him as, "This man is the divine power known as the Great Power" (Acts 8:10). He may have assumed the status of a village witchdoctor, who was more or less "a local champion," a celebrity of some sort, to use the Nigerian term. Eusebius, the church historian, later wrote of Simon as a great magician, who deified himself bearing the inscription, *Simoni deo Sancto* (Twelftree, 7).

Philip was one of the seven deacons, who were selected to serve tables in order to help resolve the early church's problem of "food distribution" among widows (Acts 6:1). Acts 8:4-8 explains that Philip went to Samaria to preach the Gospel because of the great persecution that had arisen against the church in Jerusalem. This had led to the martyr death of Stephen. Philip came to Samaria, preached the Gospel, performed miraculous signs and people, "paid close attention to what he said and did. With shrieks, evil spirits came out of many, and many paralytics and cripples were healed" (Acts 8:6-7). Miracles and workings of healings were a continuation of Jesus' earthly ministry, which became the mark of the apostolic era.

The ministry of preaching the Kingdom of God was inextricably linked to exorcism and the working of signs and wonders. For instance, in the early church, the outpouring of the Holy Spirit enabled the apostles to exhibit elements of enablement, which created tremendous impact. In other words, Philip continued in the same mode of Jesus' ministry.

When people heard Philip preach the Gospel of the Kingdom of God, and the name of Jesus, many were baptized, both men and women. Simon followed Philip everywhere, astonished by the great signs and miracles that he saw. Verse 18 states that it was ,"when Simon saw the Spirit was given at the laying on of the apostles' hands that he offered them money." Johnson has noted that the title, "the divine power known as the Great power finds parallel in the Nag Hammadi document discovered in the 4th century in Egypt" (170). He says further:

> Simon recognized a power that was worth procuring, even at a high price. His reasoning was consistent with that of the religious professionals of his day. One hundred years after Philip's visit to Samaria, Pakebkis, son of Marsisouchus, offered 2200 drachmae to purchase the office of the prophet in the temple of Sakhebtunis (Cromus in Egypt). His written application also specified, of course, that he expected to receive 20% of the temple's revenues (Johnson, 171).

From Johnson's writing here, we see that the attraction in Samaria towards the "miraculous power" continued even after Simon's experience in this passage. Simon's request is popularly referred to today as "Simony," namely "the buying and selling of Church offices or privileges of it" (Gempf, 1079).

Simon also wanted to acquire power to attract more people, a greater name, fame and more money from his magical art, just as is the case today among some miracle workers in some Pentecostal churches. Gempf has observed, "Simon thought Christianity was essentially the same with his magic, but he was mistaken as it lacked the force of the Holy Spirit which also transforms." In fact, Johnson sees Simon's request as arising from his background which had been influenced, to some extent, with similar "pagan influences" (Johnson, 172). He says that, "for centuries the Samaritans had practiced the syncretism that Moses had condemned" (2 Kings 17:25-41) and Simon was continuing to promote that poisonous mixture (Johnson, 172). This can easily find parallels today in Nigeria, where some aspects of African Traditional Religion (such as belief in witchcraft, sorcery and divination) have been "hybridized" into some new forms of Christian practices, particularly by some ritually based workings of miracles.

Ehindero has captured this problem more succinctly thus:

> Nearly all of them (Pentecostals) preach about money today. Just listen to any of these pastors on TV on their almighty pulpit and you will see what I mean. Jesus never preached money and neither did he preach miracles. Some of them have gone into most powerful cultism to bring miracles to the unstable Christians. They create an atmosphere for miracle for them to get what they want (220).

This is why Peter, who pronounced this curse on him, condemned Simon "may your money perish with you, because you thought you could buy the gift of God with money"

(Acts 8:20). Peter describes Simon, as "full of bitterness," and captive to sin (v. 23) an allusion to Deuteronomy 29:18. The emphasis on "power show" and money has diverted people's focus today, from the real source of God's power and the regeneration influence of the Holy Spirit, which the Acts of the Apostles exemplifies.

The missionary endeavour of Philip to Samaria also deserves some comments. The fact that Philip went to Samaria to preach the Gospel and people accepted his message and followed him highlights the inclusive essence of the Gospel which does not exclude anyone due to his/her ethnic background, or other social barriers. Philip's example should provide a basis for a missionary focus in Nigeria that involves divine encounter and genuine transformation. As Kisau, notes rightly, the "conversion of Simon the sorcerer should encourage the Church to evangelize everyone in the area, including the sorcerers" (1313).

Contextualizing Acts 8:9-25

This section seeks to contextualize the text under consideration in the light of Pentecostal experience in Nigeria. The basic presupposition here derives from the conviction that the text raises issues that apply to our situation in Nigeria today. Although Pentecostalism became fervent in its spread and growth from the 1970s in Nigeria, its roots had been laid before then.

Kalu has shown how the African Independent Churches (now African Instituted Churches) AICS, broke out from the missionary (mainline) churches, with emphasis on prayer,

healing, Holy Ghost baptism, speaking in tongues, deliverance
and so on (Kalu, 164). Ojo writes:

> The most remarkable development within Nigerian
> Christianity since the Aladura revival of the 1930s is
> the emergence of the charismatic movements from the
> early 1970s. Charismatic movements have brought in
> a substantial Christian awakening in the country with
> their emergence, the creative centre of Christianity
> in shifting from the mainline Protestant and Aladura
> churches to these movements (2).

The Nigeria-Biafra Civil War of 1967-1970 provided
the opportunity for Pentecostal rise and growth. Today,
Pentecostalism has provided a brand of vibrancy to
Christianity in Nigeria, with added emphases on power
encounter, prosperity, breakthroughs and signs and wonders.
In fact, Richard Burgess has articulately documented the
Pentecostal rise and growth among "Igbo Pentecostals" from
the Civil War years in Nigeria to corroborate this assertion
(179).

The influence of globalization, occasioned by the rapid
expansion of information technology and interconnectivity,
has made Pentecostalism a media propagating faith
through "tele-evangelism" and "cyber-evangelism" using the
television, radio and the internet.

Youth involvement in the Pentecostal churches has
added great impetus to Pentecostal spread and growth. The
continuous proliferation of Pentecostal churches arises from
their abandonment of the mainline churches to establish
their own churches in order to assert some level of

independence and autonomy. Thus, they become founders, general overseers, senior pastors, Bishops and so on, further contributing to Pentecostal growth in Nigeria.

Amidst the growing trend has also emerged the promotion of popular theological viewpoints and practices, propagated by quacks, ill-prepared ministers and those who lack deep theological training and expertise in handling Biblical texts and their application. The result of this has led to the perpetration of several abuses and excesses. The term "Penterascals" has been used to describe this phenomenon. They could be referred to, also, as "charlatans," as it is used in this work.

Because of the quest for power, control and search for the miraculous, terms such as "anointing," "Holy Ghost fire," "sowing seed," "claiming or rejecting this or that," "not my portion," and "back to sender prayers" have characterized Pentecostal vocabulary. Such teaching has given rise to charlatans and provided them space to thrive.

Verse 16 mentions that Philip laid hands on the people, and they received the Holy Spirit. One of the areas that has suffered abuse, misinterpretation and misapplication today, is the emphasis on "laying of hands" and anointing. In the Old Testament, anointing was reserved specifically for priests, kings and prophets. Holy oil (olive oil), was poured over the head of a person as a sign that one was set apart for the service of God (Fleming, 19). Anointing carried with it the anointing of God (1 Sam. 10:1; 24:6) and was associated with the gift of God's power, the gift of his Spirit for specific tasks (1 Sam. 16:13). It symbolized the outpouring of God's Spirit, in equipping a person for God's service (Is. 61:1, Acts 10:38).

Jesus himself was anointed as Messiah (Lk. 4:18; Acts 4:26-27; 10:38).

According to Kisau, "the anointing through laying of hands was a special one and not a general rule" (1314). Today this text has been distorted and its application is abused and counterfeited. Anointing oil, can now be bought, diluted or even faked and sold expensively to its patronizers. In fact, the quest for anointing has led to some unhealthy use of rituals and magical practices in order to possess the powers to do miracles as Simon the magician saw and wanted to acquire. The craze for anointing and search for miracles have led to trade for human body parts, where major human parts (such as human skulls, tongues, toes and genitals) have been patronized by ritual priests, including some Pentecostals (The Nation Newspaper, 16). When people fake miracles in the name of Jesus or use magical means to perform miracles, as has been alleged of some Pentecostal churches in Nigeria, they are promoting the trade of the charlatans.

From the passage under consideration, Simon's quest for power, from the anointed hands of Philip was stimulated by his desire to acquire power to be able to anoint others in order to attract more mighty works, more people, get greater name and money for himself.

There have been accusations and suspicions among Pentecostal pastors, as to the genuineness or otherwise, of some of the miracle claims. For example, Pastor Chris Okotie, of the Household of God Church, Lagos accused Pastor Chris Oyakhilome, of the Christ Embassy, of "hibernating with the Devil, Pastor Joshua," one who is "a quintessential mystic practicing docetic Gnosticism and Corinthian heresy, who uses occultic powers" (Gwamna (a), 201). In fact, T.B. Joshua's miracles were considered by Pastor Chris Okotie, as "illusions and fraudulent" (201). Similar accusations have been made by Pastor Matthew Ashimolowo of the Kingsway International Christian Church (KICC), London "who doubts T.B. Joshua's miracles' authenticity," and accuses him of engaging in occultic practices, despite the large crowds that patronize the Church. In fact, the theatrical shows that characterize the healing sessions and "the magnetic pull" of the crowd to the healing ground add to the continuous questioning of his methods.

Pentecostals have also been alleged to be involved in very unwholesome practices, such as occultic practices, sexual immorality, financial misappropriation, murder and fake supernatural claims. Other practices include focusing on money, wealth, prosperity and tithes (Akaeze, 21). Anele, a Philosophy scholar, captures this scenario thus:

> The worst culprits really are the new Pentecostal evangelists who use all kinds of tricks, all kinds of psychological, emotional shenanigans to extort both money and material things from gullible Nigerians so that, instead of focusing on spiritual enlightenment and some of those universal values that actually promote sound community and peaceful existence, you see the Pastors extolling wealth, extrolling crude materialism so that prosperity becomes the ultimate goal of being a child of God (21).

Anele accuses some Pastors of deceiving the public, in the name of performing miracles (Akaeze, 21). Such activities are captured in some Nigerian videos that further corroborate the foregoing observation. Anele summarizes the scenario thus:

> What I saw in those vidoes captured the essence of what
> is happening in Pentecostal religion where you have
> criminals, chronic sexual perverts, people that wear
> wickedness as garments portraying themselves as men
> of God (189).

The same scenario has raised similar questions about the ministry of Rev. Emeka Ezeugo King (Rev. King), the General Overseer of Christian Praying Assembly, Lagos, who, it is alleged, has hypnotized his followers with questionable claims, and was sentenced to death having been found guilty of murder (Akaeze, 22).

The use of handkerchiefs and aprons, anointed objects such as books written by "anointed ministers," and rituals for success in business or exams have elevated miracles to the level of the "magico-exorcists" and "magico-miraculous workers," thereby reducing "miracle, for sale."

Today, because of people's search for signs and wonders, little or no interest is paid to the enabling power of the Holy Spirit that characterized early apostolic witness. To support this further, Ehindero writes that,

> . . . on the issue of pulling crowds, those claiming to
> be pulling more crowds than others are only taking
> advantage of poverty in society by promising riches
> in the shortest time. This is an attractive proposition
> considering how poor most church-goers are (221).

In other words, the living conditions of people have been exploited, which further question the Biblical conformity of such beliefs and practices.

The offer of money to buy the gift of miracles (v.19) deserves some comments, as it relates to money and trading with God's power. From the text, it is obvious that Simon must have been rich, to the extent that he offered to buy the anointing power from Philip. He mistook the grace gifts of the Holy Spirit. Therefore, his offer was opposed to apostolic tradition. Today, some have promoted similar Simonic tendencies in some churches, where they offer miracles for sale, including money for counseling, deliverance and breakthroughs and the cost is determined by the extent of need. In fact, the quest for money has been identified as a factor in the continuous mushrooming of Pentecostal churches in Nigeria. The emphasis on prosperity and wealth has elevated some churches to the level of selling God's grace, similar to the scenario which characterized the church before the Protestant Reformation of Martin Luther.

Simon's request was condemned by Peter. In v. 20, Peter answered Simon, "may your money perish with you because you thought you could buy the gift of God with money." Simon repented of his sin, in order to escape from God's wrath. This has made some people to suggest that Simon had not truly repented, in the first instance.

The indication that the Holy Spirit had not come on people, as they received Christ and were baptized, also, deserves some comment. Acts of the Apostles presented other instances, where conversions went along with the indwelling of the Holy Spirit, but it was not a general rule. This verse, therefore, has brought out the significance of an aspect of early conversion experience as a package in which repentance, baptism and the indwelling of the Holy Spirit was a complete experience that led to genuine conversion and new life.

From the foregoing, certain facts here emerged that need to be addressed:

i.   Pentecostal experience is about the Holy Spirit's empowerment;

ii.   God's miracles and other signs and wonders (including healing) are God-inspired, and should not be cajoled through inducements of money;

iii. The tendency to seek and abuse God's miraculous powers is still prevalent in our age as was demonstrated by Simon the magician;

iv.   The tendency to overlook the essential and crucial source of power, for the charismatic-miraculous show, is still being witnessed today in our age;

v.   The passage has a missionary application, in God reaching out to everyone irrespective of religious and racial backgrounds;

MacArthur has put it rightly when he notes that, "what was really crucial was that everyone present knew there were not two churches. There was only one, with the same Holy Spirit under the same apostolic authority" (182).

To underscore the significance of what he considers the "Samaritan revival" to the church, MacArthur says:

> This was no casual event. Only the occasion of the Gentiles (Ch. 10) can be compared with it. Samaria was both a bridge to be crossed and a base to be occupied. A bridge

> to be crossed because Samaria represented
> the deepest clefts: the racial-religious. A base
> to be occupied because the church no longer
> resides in Jerusalem among Jews alone, but
> becomes a mission (181).

It is from such inclusiveness of the text that we draw relevance and application here, in our African context.

vi.   Simon's miracles were used to magnify himself, while Philip's were empowered by God to glorify Christ;

vii. Simon focused on the miracles and not the message, as is being witnessed in some churches today;

viii. The Gospel has power;

ix.   The Gospel brings joy;

x.   The Gospel demands genuine repentance and high moral standards; and

xi.   Miracles can be counterfeited (see also Ex. 7:11; 8:17, Acts 16:16; 28:8-11).

Some Pentecostal preachers have become popular for their exorcist powers, namely their ability to drive out demonic attacks, perform deliverance sessions from curses and witchcraft attacks and so on. Such preachers are considered popular, as they are conceived to be filled with anointing and the power of the Holy Spirit. In some cases, those who patronize them believe that just a touch of their hands on them and lying down on the anointed ground heals them. Such charismatic shows of healing powers have also gone for a fee depending on the seriousness or otherwise of such diseases and afflictions.

Counterfeiting miracles is manipulative and is condemned in many Biblical passages. For example, in Deuteronomy 13:1-5 Moses warned against fortunetellers and dreamers who led people to worship "other gods." Jesus himself spoke of those who worked miracles without knowing him (Matt. 7:22-23). Paul mentions also workers of "fake miracles, signs and wonders" (2 Thess. 2:9 cf. 2 Cor. 11:4). As K. Neil Foster and Paul L. King, have rightly noted, "it is possible even in a context that seems to be overtly evangelical and biblical, to have binding and loosing from another 'Jesus', who is not God Almighty." They, therefore, call for testing and caution (200).

The use of the name of Jesus in order to fake miracles was known. For example, in Luke 9:49, John said to Jesus, "we saw a man driving out demons in your name and we tried to stop him, because he is not one of us." The encounter of some Jews in Ephesus, with the seven sons of Sceva, arose because they had gone around driving out evil spirits invoking the name of Jesus. Graham H. Twelftree calls them "door to door exorcists" who used the name of Jesus in their incantations, but they were fake (28). He notes further that, "there are hints as to what may have been known about exorcism by the early Christians such as Justin Martyr (ca.100-ca.165) and Jewish historian, Josephus."

Twelfree, however, indicates that, "it is suggested that Jesus' methods of exorcism are nearer those of Apollonius or that of the first century Jewish charismatic than an exorcist in the magical tradition (Twelftree, 47)."

The Acts of the Apostles is replete with conflict, regarding money and big business in the early Church. For example, Sapphira and Ananias lied against the Holy Spirit because they saved some money for themselves (Acts 5:1-11). Similarly, Paul had an encounter with the slave girl, who had a spirit and had predicted the future and made money. When she followed Paul, and Paul prayed and the spirit left her, it stirred up conflict with her owners who had used her to get money (16:16-18). Paul's encounter with Demetrius the silver smith also led to conflict in Ephesus (Acts 19:23-41).

From these passages above, therefore, it becomes obvious that it was more important, to preach the Gospel than to win the support of the wealthy and influential people, as is the case today in some of our churches.

Conclusion

The early Apostles made a mark and transformed lives, because the Holy Spirit provided power and enablement for their exploits and impact. The Holy Spirit also contributed to the apostolic successes that characterize the text of the Acts of the Apostles. Simon, the magician, and a few others, emerged in the corpus of the Acts narrative, as examples of those who saw this influence and power as something that could be obtained through cash offers, as we have sometimes witnessed in some Pentecostal churches. The tendency to attract following, fame, popularity and money, has led many miracle workers to practices that contradict the Biblical witness. Manipulation and counterfeiting miracles, which was Simon's stock in trade, has found entry in some Pentecostal churches, as the craze for signs and wonders, as well as the power quest by followers, has become a major trademark of charlatans and magicians. This calls for a shift in understanding of the Biblical paradigms regarding the issues of power, signs and wonders and Holy Spirit experience, in order to safeguard Christians from those perpetuating the abuses and counterfeiting of the miraculous power that we witness.

CHAPTER 7

THEOLOGICAL EDUCATION AND NATIONAL TRANSFORMATION IN NIGERIA

Introduction

Theological education in Nigeria has witnessed rapid and steady growth over the years. The growth of theological schools (such as Bible Colleges, Seminaries and Theological Institutes) has also posed several challenges, in regards to their relevance to churches and to nation building as a whole. This chapter argues that theological education has a significant role to play towards national transformation in Nigeria. The chapter provides historical antecedents of theological education in Africa, with contextual challenges that call for reflection in Nigeria today.

Background Information on Nigeria

A brief commentary on Nigeria evokes provocative and sad passions. Nigeria emerged as an independent nation state from British colonial rule on October 1, 1960. With a current population slightly above 160 million people, it is one of the biggest black nations in the world. Nigeria is endowed with huge human and natural resources, with the potential to emerge as one of the developed nations in the world.

It is the fifth largest producer of oil in the world. However, a look at Nigeria and at its people today portrays a nation that has lost its potential for growth. Commentators on Nigeria have described Nigeria's present state in many ways. For example, Eghosa Osaghae refers to Nigeria as a "Crippled giant" and Maeir as "This House Has Fallen" (Maeir, 16). For Adebiyi, Anglican Bishop of Lagos West Diocese, Nigeria is "Africa's sleeping giant" (Adebiyi, 75). Kukah says, "Nigeria is one kind place. Its people think one kind, and they behave one kind" (Public presentation, 4). In the words of a Nigerian pop music star, Abdulkareem Idris, "Nigeria jaga jaga, everything scatter, scatter." Nigeria is described as "a nation in decay," "a nation eaten by locusts," and "a nation that has pierced its soul." In the words of Ilechukwu, Nigeria is "a failed state that works" (Ilechukwu, 29).

Today Nigeria seems to be a country that is at war with itself as the "evil men" have literally taken over the reins of the state. The paradoxical and negative indices in Nigeria indicate a troubling scenario, when compared with other nations of the world. A few of such vital statistics show the following:

i.   For many years, Nigeria has had and still has the highest mortality in the world, particularly of maternal deaths (McCain (b), 2);

ii. Out of 182 countries ranked by the Transparency International (TI) in 2012, Nigeria was ranked 142 as one of the most corrupt nations in the world;

iii.   Since 1960 it is alleged that Nigeria has been drained of US \$400 billion by its leaders (Houston, 11);

iv.   In 2011 the UNDP, World Bank and IMF showed that Nigeria lives below its status, as the world's fifth largest producer of oil; "the only major producer of oil that is known to be abysmally poor" (Adebiyi, 7);

v.   More than 70% of Nigerians live below poverty level, namely, those who live on less than US \$1 per day (*Nigerian Tribune*, 7);

vi.   Despite its huge human and material resources, Nigeria is still plagued by natural disasters, environmental degradation, destructive accidents, diseases (such as malaria, polio, lassa fever, river blindness, etc);

vii.   Nigeria has one of the poorest people in the world, but has the highest paid leaders in the world; and

viii.   Nigeria is described as the "most religious nation in the world," and also the most corrupt nation in the world. This is what Onaiyekan calls "a nation of superlatives" (Onaiyekan, 2).

Added to the above are the systemic collapse of infrastructure, moral decay, leadership failure, lawlessness (including both among the led leaders and the law makers), whose honourable lawmakers and executive officers have gained a new acclaim as, "dishonourables" and "executhieves." Nigeria can best be compared to what Amos saw of Israel, as a people who had "turned justice into bitterness and cast righteousness to the ground" (Am. 5:7). Isaiah says, "So justice is driven back and righteousness stands at a distance, truth has stumbled in the streets, honesty cannot enter" (Is. 59:14):

a. **Insecurity**: Nigeria's security apparatus today is on trial. To say it has collapsed is not an exaggeration. The killings of *Boko Haram*, along with kidnappings, assassinations and armed gang attacks, have left Nigeria as a dreaded place and a theatre of war unprecedented in its history. Human life has lost its sacredness. The impunity, in which this has continued unabated, depicts the depths of our culture of lawlessness, in which we have found ourselves, not to mention the government's failure to provide protection for lives and property of its citizens. We seem to be experiencing a similar scenario to that of Israel, when "in those days Israel had no king, everyone did as He saw fit" (Jdg 21:25); and likened to a "city divided against itself." As Jesus said: "a city divided against itself cannot stand" (Matt. 12:25; Mk 3:25).

  The complicity of the state officials, religious leaders and of Nigerians in general, shows that Nigeria is sliding towards annihilation. Recent calls for the breakup of the country by many groups are indicators towards self-immolation. Isaiah 5:20 says: "woe to those who call evil good, and good evil, who put darkness for lights, and light for darkness, who put bitter for sweet and sweet for bitter." They are people who say "peace, peace, when there is no peace" (Jer. 6:14).

b. **Poverty**: As noted earlier, Nigeria is one of the most richly endowed nations in the world, but also has the poorest people in the world. Its people have been reduced to all forms of hunger and deprivation becoming vulnerable to all forms of societal crimes. Poverty has affected families and the church. In the words of Nigerian Afro musician, Fela Anikulapokuti, Nigerians are a "people who are suffering and smilling." Ogara supports Fela, when he also adds, "many Nigerians are more dead than alive" (51). For Adebiyi, "we have become like the cloth owner who wears rags" (48) and compared to the picture the Psalmist aptly captured of Israel, "He turned rivers into desert, flowing spring into thirsty ground, and fruitful land into a salt waste because of the wickedness of those who lived there" (Ps. 107:33-34). Today the gap between the rich and the poor is so high. By the "poor" here, "we are talking of people without food, without education, without social status, without shelter, and without hope" (Ogara, 53). The poor are the losers and the most despised in our society.

c. **Corruption**: Nigeria has been acclaimed as one of the most corrupt nations in the world. Corruption has been defined as, "the misuse of public power for private benefit." Corruption has permeated every segment of Nigeria. Adebiyi states that,

> . . . even the blind knows that Nigeria is a thoroughly corrupt country. Corruption flourishes in Nigeria today; it is endemic

> from cradle to grave. It is noticeable in
> homes, markets, government offices, private
> organizations and even in churches (Adebiyi,
> 240).

Jones has supported this observation, when he noted that corruption, through theft and kleptocracy, by the top leadership in government in order to enrich themselves and their allies, was promoted by military leaders and has continued unabated since the exit of the military in 1999 (Jones, 153). For Campbell, "ubiquitous patronage and corrupt behaviour fuelled by oil money is a root cause of Nigeria's political and economic sclerosis" (32). In fact, Campbell noted that instead of being a blessing, petroleum has produced staggering wealth for a tiny elite and Nigeria has become one of the victims of the "resource curse" (32).

Different types of corruption have been identified including:

a.   political corruption (bribery, election, rigging, nepotism, cronyism and mediocrity);

b.   educational corruption (lack of funding, payment for admissions, sex for grades, and examination malpractices);

c.   religious corruption (e.g. charging money for miracles, promoting false miracle claims and connivance with corrupt government officials);

d.   economic and financial corruption (such as bribery, inflated contracts, inducements and indiscrimate price increases) and

e.   corruption in public and private sectors.
When the church keeps silent and stammers in the face of injustice and societal vices, it is corruption. When the church exploits people, who are already poverty-stricken, and preaches only a prosperity message for gain, it is corruption. When men and women of God (ministers of God) fail to preach and to lead their people well, it is corruption. When Christians collaborate with evil men to perpetuate evil, it is corruption.

The Bible condemns corruption. Ecclesiastes 7.7 says, "Extortion turns a wise man into a fool, and a bribe corrupts the heart." Exodus 23:8 says: "Do not accept a bribe for a bribe; it blinds those who see and twist the compensation however great it is." Corruption affects development. In fact, Nigeria's lack of development and other socio-political and economic woes are directly attributable to the evils of corruption.

d.   **False Spirituality**: Nigeria is a religious nation and with a highly conscious religious people. The external religious symbols seen in the show of religiosity in the public space, portray the validity of this observation. Nigeria's religiosity has been criticized as a mere external show of religion and spirituality, similar to the Pharisaic posturing of

Jesus' day that he condemned. Jesus condemned the Pharisees "who do not practice what they preach" (Matt. 23:3). Similarly, the church in Nigeria has become infected with the virus of corruption. Akinwale stated, "Nigeria is polluted by toxic fumes issuing from a deadly mixture of corrupt politics and corrupt religion" (16).

The church has become part of Nigeria's problem. We are witnesses today of the false ministers of God, who masquerade as angels of light but are wolves in sheep's clothing (2 Cor. 11:14). We have miracle merchants, magicians and charlatans who, in the name of "anointing," have cheated an unsuspecting public. The new wave of acquisition of private jets by some Nigerian church leaders despite the abject poverty-striken condition of most people, has become, in the words of Kukah, not only "embarrassing and deplorable," but has "diminished the moral voice of the church" (4). In the name of God today, religious extremists have perpetuated religious intolerance, crime and condemnable acts. Ogara notes that, "in God's name a lot of evils ranging from the bizarre to the profane, are committed on a daily basis. Stories abound in every minute of every day" (Ogara, 125). Mahatma Ghandi cautioned that, "oppression of people in the name of God is the worst form of oppression" (Ogara, 127).

Old Testament prophets and Jesus himself condemned false religion that dehumanized people (Matt. 23:4). In the words of Archbishop A. Obinna of Owerri, "those called to be fishers of men have become hookers of men; hooking people to sin, using all kinds of tricks." It is of such scenarios as this that the Psalmist asked in Psalm 11:3, "when the foundations are destroyed, what will the righteous do?" Such a dilemma calls for a national transformation in Nigeria today.

The Need for a National Transformation

"National transformation" has become a popular catchword in Nigeria's public space. According to Oyemakinde:

> Transformation is a complete change. It denotes about-turn, total twist or full scale, full circle. Transformation is about turning over to a new leaf, a new life, a new order, a new way, a new style, a new strategy, a new look, a new view, a new focus, a novel dispensation (1)

Transformation involves an experience of a new beginning. It involves abandoning things that are no longer valuable or relevant. The emphasis of transformation is on rebirth, just as Paul said: "therefore if anyone is in Christ, he is a new creation, old things have passed away, behold, all things have become new" (2 Cor. 5:17). Christians are a transformed people who are expected to transform their society. When Jesus told his disciples that, "you are the salt of the earth", and the "light of the world" (Matt. 5:13-14) it was a call to be agents and catalysts of transformation in their society. As Stetzer and Rainer have observed, we treasure the concept of 'transformation' because radical change is the heart of the Christian message, and because the power of the gospel changes everything-lives, churches and communities (1)

God has called us to make a transformational impact on the world. The Gospel is its power and it bears fruit. Paul confirms this when he said, "all over the world, this Gospel is bearing fruit and growing" (Col. 1:16). Wherever the Gospel has been preached and accepted, it has brought transformation. The history of world revivals and the Reformation created transformed lives and nations around the world. Paul said in Romans 12:2:

> Do not be conformed any longer to the pattern of this world, but be transformed by the renewing of your mind. Then, you will be able to test and approve what God's will is – his good, pleasing and perfect will.

The transformation of God brings freedom from sin, rigid legalism and hopelessness. This is achieved through the Spirit of God. Zechariah 4:6 says this is achieved, "not by strength or by might, but my Spirit says the Lord of Hosts."

Nevertheless, certain questions become necessary for our further reflection namely:

i.   How can there be national transformation, when the bulk of Nigerians are unpatriotic, corrupt and indolent?

ii.   How can there be national transformation, when the leadership is corrupt?

iii.   How can there be national transformation, when our national programs towards transformation are devoid of God's standards?

iv. How can there be national transformation, when
     some of our religious leaders have also joined the
     bandwagon of corrupt Nigerians?

National transformation cannot take place in Nigeria, until
its people experience a national cleansing of the heart, a
cleansing which comes from God. He gives power and the
transformational will to achieve this. Second Chronicles 7:14
says,

> "If my people who are called by my name will humble
> themselves and pray and seek my face, and turn from
> their wicked ways, then I will hear from heaven and
> will forgive their sin and will heal their land."

In a country like Nigeria where wickedness has reached
unprecedented heights, only humble submission to God in
repentance can bring forgiveness and healing in the land. In a
country that has suffered division, ethnic strife and religious
conflicts, only God's healing can restore the land and bring
reconciliation and peace.

We can learn some models from Jesus and the Bible for
application here, namely:

i.   Jesus sent out his disciples to the world to touch lives
      (Lk. 9:1-2).

ii.   Jesus had a heart for people and he reached out
      to them irrespective of their social and religious
      background (Jn. 4).

iii. Jesus surrounded himself with lost people (Lk. 15.1).
      He related with tax collectors and sinners, was kind
      to the adulterous woman (Jn. 8:1-11) and Zachaeus,

the tax collector (Lk. 9:1-10). By offering grace and truth, the lost were drawn to Him to be changed.

iv. Jesus felt the needs of the people (Jn. 11:35, Matt. 9: 35-37); he fed the hungry (Matt. 15: 29), and took time for the people (Mk. 10: 51).

v.   Jesus came to serve the hurting (Lk. 4: 18) and to save the lost (Lk. 19:10). In Him we witness the greatest transformational leadership skills the world has ever known.

vi. Jesus identified with the people (Mk. 2:15).

vii. Jesus showed excellence in ministry. Mark 7:37 says: "people were overwhelmed with amazement and exclaimed, 'he has done everything well.'" Danny McCain has noted, ". . . if there is any quality that should characterize Christians, it should be the quality of excellence." To McCain (c), "we should be excellent because God is excellent" and has provided the Biblical basis for excellence (see Ps. 8, Dan. 6:3, Phil. 4:8) (28). Colossians 3:23 says, "whatever you do, work at it with your heart, as working for the Lord."

viii. Jesus took time for people (Mk. 10.51) and served with humility (Matt. 23:12).

Transformational leaders need to reach out beyond their confines. Bob Briner and Ray Pritchard observe that:

> Peter, James and John did not become able
> leaders by lingering in Caparnaum on the Sea

> of Galilee, but by traveling to Jerusalem . . .
> Leaving home is part of God's plan for our
> leadership (82).

ix. Transformational leadership mentors. Paul says: "and the things you have heard me say in the presence of many witnesses, entrust to reliable people who will also be qualified to teach others" (2 Tim. 2:2). Other Biblical examples abound:

    a. Moses mentored Joshua (Num. 14, 26, Jos. 14, 15).
    b. David mentored Solomon (1 Chron. 29:19).
    c. Elijah mentored Elisha (2 Kings 2).
    d. Jesus mentored the disciples (Mk. 1:17).
    e. Paul mentored Timothy and Titus (2 Tim. 1:2, Tit. 1:4).

We need leaders today, who will mentor the young ones with values that will transform Nigeria in the next generation.

x. Transformation leadership promotes unity. Jesus says, "If a house is divided against itself, that house cannot stand." We need ministers today, who will promote unity in the church and not ethnic warlords in ministry who promote ethnicity and division (1 Cor. 3. 1ff.).

Theological Education in Nigeria

Walls has observed that, "in the past half-century, the theological map of the world has been transformed" (16).

With the global shift of Christianity toward the South, and the growing influence of Christianity, particularly in Nigeria, the task of theological education has become enormous. Theological education provides men and women a sound, biblically based theology, that will contribute to God's kingdom here on earth and enables them to significantly impact their respective societies. Theological education exposes one to the foundations of basic theological training, discipline and God's mandate, as captured by Paul in 2 Timothy 2:15, namely, "Do your best to present yourself to God as one approved, a workman who does not need to be ashamed and who correctly handles the word of truth."

Walls notes that, "theology is a dangerous business, an act of intellectual adoration of the living God fraught with the risk of blasphemy" (26). Theological education provides alternative God-centered and Christ-oriented principles for living in such a society that has lost its Godly values as Nigeria.

Africa has had a rich theological history and legacy. Africa produced theological giants in Augustine, Origen, Tertullian, Justin, and Cyprian, among others. Their theological formulations and Biblical interpretation shaped early Christianity. For example, the Catechetical school, the first of its kind in the world, founded at Alexandria, Egypt in 180AD, was the first theological institution in early Christianity. For Thomas C. Oden, "Africa was the sweet kernel of the grain that fed Christian intellectual history before Constantine." Indeed "African Christianity in the early centuries served as the intellectual powerhouse of early Christian thinking" (Oden, 14).

The challenges of theological education in Nigeria are enormous. They range from training and retention of staff, maintaining theological balance and evangelical tradition amidst a highly proliferated church and ministries; recruitment of students who have been called to ministry, funding (to pay staff, develop physical facilities, develop a library), and a theological curriculum that will help to address societal problems such as in Nigeria. Because of these challenges, some theological schools and Bible colleges still depend on overseas grants and scholarships to fill this vacuum. With the current national awakening concerning the need of theological education one cannot emphasize highly enough the need to address these issues.

Theological education has contributed, in no small measure, to nation building in Nigeria. It has produced manpower for engagement in the church and in the larger Nigerian society. To this extent, theological education has supplemented the government, in the face of the dearth of adequate funding in the education sector and addressing unemployment. It has raised men and women with kingdom values, who are contributing in many ways to the national agenda of transformation.

Challenges of Application

Several challenges have been identified and discussed as pathways towards national transformation in Nigeria. They have been divided into theological and spiritual challenges:

a. **Theological Challenges**
    i.   The need for a curriculum review. The curriculum used in Nigerian theological

education needs reviewed to take into account contemporary developments and global realities. Theological responses are needed to such issues as, ethno-religious conflicts, religious fundamentalism, ethnicity and identity, the church and development, entrepreneurial studies, Christian mission in a globalised world, inter-religious dialogue and relations with people of other faiths. All these call for a contextual approach towards doing theology in Africa in order to address existential realities of the people.

A shift is needed from the typical Western theological approach that poses questions and answers that do not address Africa's theological concerns. Instead, African theological propositions and engagement needs to return to the early African engagement with Christianity, rather than be absorbed into some western liberal theology that poses great challenges to African Christianity.

ii. The need for funding of theological education in Nigeria: Because of the important role of theological education today in Nigeria, adequate funding of this sector cannot be over-emphasized. Therefore, churches and government are called upon to fund theological education in Nigeria adequately. Theological education should be properly recognized, and theologians incorporated into national efforts towards transformation. Government and NGOs could fund conferences and responses to conflicts and peace in Nigeria, where the role of religious leaders can particularly be addressed.

The renewed funding will help to address library development, recruitment and retention of qualified staff, improvement of existing facilities and living conditions generally.

iii. Theological institutions should collaborate (partner) with other institutions and research centers, in order to maintain standards and to meet the new status of leading global Christianity in a Biblically sound and universally acceptable way. This involves sharing experiences, exchanging new models of administering theological education and exploring how to confront the challenges of theological education in Nigeria.

iv. The public, including individuals and churches, are called upon to support theological education. They could institute fellowships, awards or scholarships in areas, such as pastoral ministry, counseling, church planting, Christian ethics and so on.

b. **Spirituality Challenges**

i. We need to repent and turn from our evil ways of doing things, if we truly want national transformation. Proverbs 14:34 says, "righteousness exalts a nation, but sin is a disgrace to any people." Isaiah 32:17 says, "the fruit of righteousness will be peace, the effect of righteousness will be quietness and confidence forever." Malachi 4:2 says, "But for you who revere my name, the sun of righteousness will rise with healing in its wings. And you will go out and leap like calves released from the stall." Psalm 127:1 also says, "unless the Lord builds the house, its builders labour in vain."

ii.	True national transformation requires that we seek and do justice in church and society, in both private and public life. Amos 5:24 says, "But let justice roll like a river, righteousness like a never-failing stream." Because of injustice, Nigeria has experienced conflicts, protests and social discontent that have developed into our present experience.

iii.	Nigerians need to develop transformation values. For Nigeria to attain national transformation, we need to develop Biblical principles of hard work, integrity, service, truth, accountability, and love. These attributes have developed nations such as Malaysia, Brazil, China, Japan, Indonesia, and South Korea among others.

iv.	We need to engage in a ministry of reconciliation. We have been called to ministry with a message of reconciliation (2 Cor. 5:19). Nigeria needs reconciliation today in the aftermath of ethnic strife, religious killings, political conflicts and socio-economic deprivations that have alienated the bulk of Nigerians. Reconciliation is a way to peace in Nigeria.

v.   Nigerians need ministers of God, (pastors particularly), to stir up national revival towards transformation. This requires that pastors engage in sermons that transform, not leaving listeners unchanged. We need messages today that will preach hope and restoration, like the prophets of old (cf. Am. 9:11; Hos. 14:4; Is 61: 3-4). We need men to join in the prophetic vanguard and become like the "sons of the prophets" of old, who were watchmen and vanguards of transformation. They were vanguards, who responded to the challenges of apostasy, political instability and economic decay during their time (see 1 Sam.10:5, 1 Sam. 19:18-24, 2 Kings 2:3). They had a positive impact on their people. Oladejo depicts them as "men with discernment, vision and thirst for expansion and positive transformation." Such are the leaders that we need today in our churches in Nigeria, to lead in national transformation.

vi. Provide leadership towards transformation and not for personal gain (2 Cor. 2:17; 4:2).

vii. Transformational leadership needs to get engaged in what Yusufu Ameh Obaje calls the "politics of redemption." For Christians to effectively contribute to the transformation agenda in Nigeria, they need to engage in politics. Obaje rightly observes,

> . . . the truth of the matter is that, politics properly understood, is the main mission of the church and for the church in Africa or more especially in Nigeria- today, politics is the forgotten mission of the church.

By politics of redemption, is implied the salvific action of God that demonstrates his control and power over creation as its maker and sustainer. The politics of redemption requires that we get into God's mandate of subduing the earth and taking dominion of the affairs of men, from those who have engaged in it and have made it a "dirty game." The politics of redemption involves reclaiming Jesus' command to be salt of the earth and light of the world. It calls for commitment, vision and God-centered strategies. This is the response of the righteous to the question raised by the Psalmist in Psalm 11:3, "when the foundations are being destroyed, what can the righteous do"?

Conclusion

True and lasting national transformation comes only through righteousness that is God centered and Christ oriented. Proverbs 14:34 says, "righteousness exalts a nation, but sin is a disgrace to any people." National transformation can be achieved in Nigeria today, through a spirituality that is devoid of the hypocritical pretensions that we have witnessed in Nigeria. Instead, Nigeria needs a cleansing of the heart. Theological education has a major role to play, today, in redirecting our focus and goals towards national transformation.

WORKS CITED

Adamo, D.T., *Africa and the Africans in the Old Testament*, Justice Jeco Press, Benin City, 2005.

Adamo, D.T. *Exploration in African Biblical Studies*, Justice Jeco Press, Benin City, 2005.

Adamo, David T. "Evolving a Biblical Hermeneutics for Social Change and Transformation in Africa," A Paper Presented at the NABIS Confrence, Kogi State University, Ayingba, 2010.

Adebiyi, P.A., *Let the Nations Hear*, The Book Company, Lagos, 2012.

Adedeji, F., "Musical Revolution in Contemporary Christianity." Ogungbile, David O. and Akinade, E. Akintunde E. (ed.). *Creativity and Change in Nigerian Christianity*, 2010.

Adeleye, F., *Preachers of A Different Gospel*. Bukuru: Hippo Books, 2011.

Ademiluka, S.O., "The Use of Imprecatory Psalms in African Context," *African Journal of Biblical Studies*, Vol. Xxiii, No. II, Oct. 2006.

Adewole, S., "Charismatic Movement and Pentecostalism." *Tradition and Compromises: Essays on Challenge of Pentecostalism.* Dominican Institute, Ibadan, 2004.

Adogame, A., "Reconfiguring the Global Religious Economy: The Role of African Pentecostalism," Donald E. Miller, Kimon H. Sargeant, Richard D. Flory (Eds.), *Spirit and Power: The Growth and Global Impact of Pentecostalism*, Oxford University Press, Oxford, 2013.

Ajibade, E.A., "Anointing the Sick With Oil: An Exegetical Study of James 5:14-15" in *Ogbomoso Journal of Theology*, Vol. XIII (2), 2008.

Akaeze, A., "Woeful Men of God," *Tell*, March 3, 2014.

Akinwale, A., "Denunciation, Deconstruction and Reconstruction: Theology at the Service of Church and Society," *Ogbomosho Journal of Theology*, Vol. XVI, No. 3, 2011.

Anderson A., "Pentecostalism in Africa: An Overview." *Orita.* Ibadan: XXXVI 1-2, 2004.

__________, *An Introduction to Pentecostalism: Global Charismatic Christianity*, Cambridge University Press, 2004.

__________, *Spreading Fires: The Missionary Nature of Early Pentecostalism*, Orbis Books, Maryknoll, 2007.

Anderson, A.H., "The Emergence of a Multi-dimensional Global Missionary Movement," Donald E. Miller, Kimon H. Sargeant, Richard D. Flory (Eds.), *Spirit and Power: The Growth and Global Impact of Pentecostalism*, Oxford University Press, Oxford.

"Anthropologist's View," *Missiology: An International Review*, Vol. V. No.4, 1977.

Anyanwu, C.A. *The Relevance of Pentecostalism to the African Society: A Socio-religious Analysis*, Greenleaf Global Enterprises, Owerri, 2004.

Asaju, D.F., "Noise, Fire and Flame: Anointing and Breakthrough Phenomena among Nigerian Evangelicals." David, O. Ogungbile and Akintunde E. Akinade (ed.). *Creativity and Change in Nigerian Christianity*, 2010.

Awoniyi, R.P., "Charismatic Movements Appropriation of Indigenous Spirituality in Nigeria," *Ogbomoso Journal of Theology*, Vol. XIII (2), 2008.

Ayegboyin, D., "The Experience of New Pentecostal Movements in Nigeria," Anthony Akinwale and Joseph Kenny, *Tradition and Compromises: Essays on the Challenges of Pentecostalism*, The Michael J. Demsey Centre, Ibadan, 2004.

__________, "... But Deliver us From Evil: The Riposte of the MFM and its Implications for the Reverse in Mission" *Orita*, Vol. XXX vii, 2005.

__________, "Rethinking of Prosperity Teaching in the New Pentecostal Churches in Nigeria," *Black Theology*, Vol. 4 (1) Queens Foundation, Birmingham, 2006.

Barclay, W., *Introduction to John and the Acts of the Apostles*, The Westminster Press, Philadelphia, 1976.

Bird, M.F., *A Bird's Eye View of Paul: The Man, His Mission and His Message*, Inter-Varsity Press, Nottingham, 2008.

Blair, P.A., "Gentiles," J.D. Douglas (eds.), *New Bible Dictionary*, Inter-Varsity Press, Illinois, 1996.

Briner, B. and R. Pritchard, *The Leadership Lessons of Jesus*, B and H Publishing Group, Nashville, 2008.

Bruce, F.F., (ed.), *The International Bible Commentary*, Zondervan Publishing House, Grand Rapids, 1986.

Burgess, R., *Nigeria's Christian Revolution: The Civil War Revival and its Pentecostal Progeny (1967-2006)*, Paternoster Press, Carlisle, 2008.

Campbell, J., *Nigeria: Dancing on the Brink*, Bookcraft, Ibadan, 2010.

Chester, Tim and Steve Timmis, *Total Church: A Radical Reshaping Around Gospel and Community*, Inter-Varsity Press, Nottingham, 2007.

Chidili, Bartholomew Udealo, *Pedagogy of Human Dignity-Through the Vision of Mercy Amba Oduyoye*, Fab Educational Books, Jos, 2008.

CRUDAN News Bulletin – April-June, No.63, 2008, Oct – December No. 65, 2008; April-June No.67, 2009.

"Church Empires, Their Billions, Their Assets, Their Scandals," *Newswatch*, August 27, 2007.

Coe, S., "Contextualizing Theology," Gerald H. Anderson and Thomas F. Stransky (eds), *Mission Trends, No. 31, Third World Theologies*, Paulinist Press, New York, 1976.

Cole, Victor, "Africanizing the Faith: Another Look at the Contextualization of Theology," Samuel Ngewa et al (eds) *Issues in African Christian Theology*, East African Educational Publishers, Nairobi, 1998.

Concise Edition Dictionary and Thesaurus, Geddes and Grosset, Glasgow, 2002.

Corrie, J., "Mission and Contextualization," www.trinity_bris.ac.uk/.../Corrie_missi_an_contextualization.pdf. Date retrieved, 5th July, 2012.

Cox, H., *Fire From Heaven: The Rise of Pentecostal Spirituality and the Reshaping of Religion in the Twenty-First Century*, Da Capo Press, Cambridge, 1995.

"Culture," http://www.tamu.edu/faculty/choudhury/culture.html, p.1. Date retrieved 15th September, 2011.

Dedji, Valentin, *Reconstruction and Renewal in African Christian Theology*, Acton Publishers, Nairobi, 2003.

Dibelius, M. *Paul*, Westminister Press, Philadelphia, 1960.

Doriani, D.M., *Putting the Truth to Work: The Theory and Practice of Biblical Application*, P&R Publishing, Phillipsburg, 2001.

__________, *The Sermon on the Mount: The Character of Discipline*, P&R Publishing, Phillipsburg, 2006.

Ehindero, S.B., *The Church Idols of Our Time, Vine Message International*, Ibadan, 2010.

Ehusani, G.O., *An Afro-Christian Vision Ozovehe!: Toward a More Humanized World*, University Press of America, Lanham, 1991.

Ekenna, G., "Who Do They Serve?," in "Miracle Workers: New Generation Pastors Turn Churches into Money Making Ventures," *Newswatch*, December, 2001.

Essien, O., "Youths and Pentecostalism." David O. Ogungbile and Akintunde E. Akinade, (ed.). *Creativity and Change in Nigerian Christianity*. Malthouse Press Limited, Lagos, 2010.

Excerpts of a song from a video-CD of Okeke, Princess Oluchi, *Battle Praise*, Vol. 2, undated.

"Exploring Africa – Christianity in Africa," http://exploringafrica.matrix.msu.edu/students/curriculum/m14/activity... p.3. Date retrieved, 16th September, 2011.

Ferguson, S.B., *The Sermon on the Mount*, The Banner of Truth Trust, Edinburgh, 2006.

Fleming, D., *World's Bible Dictionary*, World Bible Publishers, Iowa, 1990.

Flemming, D., *Contextualization in the New Testament: Patterns for Theology and Mission*, Inter-Varsity Press, Illinois, 2005.

Flemming, Dean, "Contextualizing the Gospel in Athens: Paul's Areopagus Address as a Paradigm for Missionary Communication," *Missiology, An International Review*, Vol. XXX, No.2, 2002.

Flory, R., and Sargeant, K.H., "Pentecostalism in Global Perspective," Richard D. Flory (Eds.), *Spirit and Power: The Growth and Global Impact of Pentecostalism*, Oxford University Press, Oxford, 2013.

Foster, John, *The First Advance: Church History AD 29-500*, SPCK, London, 1972.

Foster, K.N. & L.K. *Paul, Binding and Loosing: Exercising Authority Over Dark Powers*, Evangel Publication, Kaduna, 1998.

Fuller, W.H., *Run While the Sun is Hot*, SIM Publications, Jos, 1967.

Gaiya, M.A.B., "Profiling Pentecostal and Charismatic Groups in Nigeria," A Research Report Presented at the Nigerian Centre for Pentecostal and Charismatic Studies Conference, at Abuja, 23-27th May, 2012.

Gehman, R., *African Traditional Religion in the Light of the Bible*, Africa Christian Textbooks, Bukuru, 2001.

Gempf, C., "Acts," D.A. Carson and R.F. France et al (eds.), *New Bible Commentary*, Inter-varsity Press, Leicester; 2007.

Getz, G.A., *Paul: Living for the Call of Christ*, B & H Publishing Group, Nashville, 2000.

Gilliland, Dean S., (ed.), *The Word Among Us: Contextualizing Theology For Mission Today*, Word Publishing, Dallas.

_______ *Pauline Theology and Mission Practice*, Baker Book House, Grand Rapids.

Gundry, R., *Matthew: A Commentary on His Literary and Theological Art*, Eerdmans, Grand Rapids, 1982.

Guthrie, Donald, *New Testament Theology*, InterVarsity Press, Illinois, 1981.

Gwamna, D.J. (a), "Divine Healing Within Pentecostalism: A Biblical Evaluation From An African Perspective," An Unpublished Ph.D Thesis, University of Jos, 2006.

Gwamna, D.J. (b), *Gbagyi Names: Religious and Philosophical Connotations*, Mazlinks, Jos, 1996.

Gwamna, D.J. (c), *Perspectives in African Theology, Africa Christian Textbooks*, Bukuru, 2008.

Gyadu, J.K.A., *African Charismatics: Current Developments within Independent Indigenous Pentecostalism in Ghana*, Brill, Leiden, 2005.

________"Born of Water and the Spirit," *Pentecostal/Charismatic Christianity in Africa*, Brill, Leiden, 2004.

Hall, D.R., "Athens," J.D. Douglas et al. (eds.), *New Bible Dictionary*, Inter-Varsity Press, Leicester, 2007.

Herr, E.G., "Salt," Geoffrey W. Bomiley (ed.), The International Standard Bible Encyclopedia, Vol. 3, Eerdmans, Grand Rapids, 1986.

Hesselgrave, D.J. "Great Commission Contextualization," www.ijfm.org/PDFs/JFN/12_3_PDFS//06. Date retrieved, 6th July, 2012.

Hornby, A.S., *Oxford Advanced Learner's Dictionary*, Oxford University Press, Oxford, 2006.

Houston, B., "The Paradox of Impoverished Africa," *Ogbomosho Journal of Theology*, (OJOT), Vol. XIV, 2009.

http://www.orthodoxwiki.org/salt_in_the_Bible, p.5. Date retrieved, 18th October, 2008.

Idowu, B., *Olodumare: God in Yoruba Belief*, Longman, Ikeja,1962.

Ilechukwu, C., *Transformational Leadership*, Fourthman Creations, Lagos, 2011.

Iwe, N.N.S., *Christianity, Culture and Colonialism in Africa*, Department of Religious Studies, College of Education, Port Harcourt, 1979.

Jenkins, P., *The New Faces of Christianity: Believing the Bible in the Global South*, Oxford University Press, Oxford, 2006.

Johnson, B., "The Godfella and the Thieves," in "Pastor of Thieves: How Oyakhilome Received Another Stolen Money," *The News*, 9th June, 2003.

Johnson, B., 'Super-Rich Godfellas,' in "Nigeria's Three Richest Pastors: Their Businesses and Influences," *The News*, 19 June, 2006.

Johnson, D.E., *The Message of Acts in the History of Redemption*, P&R Publishing, Phillipsburg, 1997.

Jones, P.C., *My Nigeria: Five Decades of Independence*, Palgrave Macmillan, New York, 2010.

Keener, C.S., *IVP Bible Background Commentary, New Testament*, Inter-Varsity Press, Downers Grove, 1993.

Keller, W.P., *Salt for Society*, Word Books, Texas, 1981.

Kenney, *Joseph, West Africa and Islam*, Dominican Press, Ibadan, 2004.

Kisau, P.M., "Acts of the Apostles," Tokunboh Adeyemo (ed.), *Africa Bible Commentary*, Word Alive Publishers, Nairobi, 2006.

Kombo, Ronald Kisilu, "Witchcraft: A Living Vice in Africa," *Africa Journal of Evangelical Theology*, Vol. 22. 1, 2003.

Kraemer, Hendrik, *Religion and the Christian Faith*, Westminster Press, Philadelphia, 1959.

Kukah, M.H., "Pastors With Private Jets an Embarrassment – Bishop Kukah," *The Nation* on Sunday, Nov. 18 2012.

______ A Public Presentation in Abuja, 2012.

Kunhiyop, Samuel Waje, *African Christian Ethics*, Hippo Books, Bukuru, 2008.

Laing, Mark, "The Changing Face of Mission: Implications for the Southern Shift in Christianity," *Missiology: An International Review*, Vol. XXXIV. No.2. April, 2006.

Land, S.J., *Pentecostal Spirituality: A Passion for the Kingdom/*, Sheffield Academic Press, Sheffield, 1994.

"Living in Bondage," *Tell*, August 23, 2004; "The Patrons of Okija Shrine," *Newswatch*, October 11, 2004; "The Killer Shrines of Igboland," *The News*, No. 7. 23, August 2004.

MacArthur, J.F., *Charismatic Chaos*, Oasis International Ltd, 1992.

Maeir, K., *This House Has Fallen*, Penguin Books, London, 2000.

Marshall, R., *Political Spiritualities: The Pentecostal Revolution in Nigeria*, The University of Chicago, Chicago Press, 2009.

Matthew Henry's Commentary on the Whole Bible, Vol. 5, Matthew – John, Hendrickson, 1994.

Matthew, Michael, *Christian Theology and African Traditions*; Yuty Graphics, Kaduna, 2011.

Mbiti, J.S., *Bible and Theology in African Christianity*, Oxford University Press, Nairobi, 1986.

Mbiti, John S., *African Religions and Philosophy*, Heinemann, Nairobi, 1969.

______ "The Dialogue between African Religion and Christianity," http:// benbyerly.wordpress.com/ 2010/05/25/ John_Mbiti-the-dialogue. Date retrieved, 16th September, 2011.

McCain, D. (a), "Church in Societal Transformation", A Paper Presented to Africa Forum on Religion and Government (AFREG) Conference on 3rd March 2010 in Abuja.

(b)______ "Mission in a Troubled World: Challenging the Church in Africa to Respond," A Paper Presented at the Theological Educators in Africa (TEA) Conference, TCNN, Bukuru, May 2012.

(c)______ *Go in and Possess the Land*, IICS Global Scholars Monograph Series, Jos 2010.

(d)______ *Notes on Acts of the Apostles*, Africa Christian Textbooks, Bukuru 2001.

(e)______ Interview with Pastor Sam Adeyemi in Lagos, 9th June 2011.

Metuh, E.I., "African Worldviews as 'Praeparatio Evangelica': An Appraisal," *The Nigerian Journal of Theology*, 1:3, 1987.

______ *God and Man in African Religion*, Chapman, London, 1981.

______ *Gods in Retreat: Continuity and Discontinuity in African Religions*, Imico Press, Enugu, 1986.

Miller, D.E., "Pentecostalism as Global Phenomenon," Donald E. Miller, Kimon H. Sargeant, Richard D. Flory (Eds.), *Spirit and*

Power: The Growth and Global Impact of Pentecostalism, Oxford University Press, Oxford, 2013.

Morris, L., "Light", in ISBE, Revised Edition; PC Study Bible, V5.

Mounce, R.H., "Sermon on the Mount", in *International Standard Bible Encyclopedia* (ISBE), Revised Edition, PC Study Bible V5.

Mugambi, J.N.K., "Challenges to African Scholars in Biblical Hermeneutics," J.N.K. Mugambi and Johannes A. Smit, *Text and Context in New Testament Hermeneutics*, Acton Publishers, Nairobi, 2004.

Musa, D., *Christians in Politics; How Can They Be Effective*, ACTS, Bukuru – Jos, 2009.

Needham, N.R., *2000 Years of Christ's Power Part One: The Age of the Early Church Fathers*, Grace Publications Trust, London, 2002.

Nickerson, L.A., "Origin and meaning of 'salt of the earth,'" http://www.humanities360.com/index.php/origin-and-meaning-of-salt-of-the-earth-5-64363/ Date retrieved 18th October 2008.

"Nigeria: New Human Development Report", http://allafrica.com/stories/201003100625.html, Date retrieved, 14th February, 2014.

Nkwalla, A., "Contextualization and African Pentecostal Mission," www.antsonline.org/article2v2il.htm, Date retrived, 12th November, 2012.

Oden, T.C., *How Africa Shaped the Christian Mind*, IVP Books, Illinois, 2007.

O'Donovan, Wilbur, *Biblical Christianity in Modern Africa*, Paternoster Press, Calisle, 2000.

Ogara, P.I., *Nigeria Must Survive*, Life Apostolate Publications, Enugu, 2011.

Ojo, M.A. *The End–Time Army: Charismatic Movements in Modern Nigeria*, Africa World Press, Trenton, 2006.

Olabimtan, K., "Mission Theory and Practice," *Ogbomosho Journal of Theology*, vol. xv (1), 2010.

Oleka, S., "The Living God: Reflections on Acts 17 and African Traditional Religions", Samuel Ngewa, Mark Shaw and Tite

Tienou, *Issues in African Christian Theology*, East African Educational Publishers Ltd, Nairobi, 1998.

Olushola, M.J., "Pentecostalism in Nigeria: Exploiting or Edifying the Masses?" *African Sociological Review* 8:2, 2004.

Omenyo, C., "The Spirit-Filled Goes to School: Theological Education in African Pentecostalism," *Ogbomoso Journal of Theology*, Vol. XIII (2) 2008.

Onaiyekan, J., "Dividends of Religion in Nigeria," Public Lecture Delivered at the University of Ilorin, 12 May, 2010.

Oyemakinde, W., *Transformation, Sunlight Syndate Ventures*, Ibadan, 2012.

Parshall, Phil, *New Paths in Muslim Evangelism: Evangelical Approaches to Contextualization*, Baker Book House, Grand Rapids, 1980.

"Patrons of Okija Shrine," *Newswatch* October 11, 2004.

Pierli, F., "The History of the Institute of Social Ministry," in Fritz Stenger (ed.), *Africa is Not a Dark Continent*, Tangaza Occasional Papers/No. 17, Paulines Publications Africa, Nairobi, 2005.

Pobee, John S., "The Search for a Living Church in Africa," Masamba ma Mpolo, et al (eds.), *An African Call for Life*, WCC, Geneva, 1983.

Polland, E.B., "Covenant of Salt," "Salt, Salt Covenant," http://www.biblereferencegiude.com/keywords/salt.convenant.html, p.3. Date retrieved, 18th October, 2008.

Reed D.A., "Acts 17:16-34 in an African Context: An Assessment from a N. Atlantic/Western Perspective," *Africa Journal of Evangelical Theology*, Vol. 22. 1, 2003.

Richards, E.R. *Paul and First Century Letter Writing*, Inter-Varsity Press, Illinois, 2004.

"Salt in the Bible," "What does the Bible say About Magic, Magicians, Illusionists?,"http://www.gotquestions.org/magic-illision-Bible.html, p.1. Date retrieved, 8th May, 2010.

Sanneh, L., "Renewed and Empowered: The Christian Impact," *Ogbomosho Journal of Theology*, Vol. XV (1) 2010.

________ *Whose Christianity? The Gospel Beyond the West,* Eerdmans Publishing Company, Grand Rapids, 2003.

Sider, R.J., *Good News and Good Works: A Theology for the Whole Gospel,* Baker Books, Grand Rapids, 2004.

"Simon Peter versus Simon the Sorcerer or Peter Meets the Competition II," http://www.reformation.org/simon peter versus Simon Magus.html.

Stetzer, E. and Rainer, T.S., *Transformational Church,* B and H Publishing Group, Nashville, 2010.

Storms, C.S., *Healing and Holiness: A Biblical Response to Faith Healing Phenomenon,* P&R Publishing Company, Phillipsburg, 1990.

Stott, J., *Christian Mission in the Modern World,* IVP, Downers Grove, 1975.

Taylor, J.V., *The Primal Vision: Christian Presence Amid African Religion,* SCM Press, London 1963.

Twelftree, G.H., *In the Name of Jesus: Exorcism Among Early Christians,* Baker Academic, Grand Rapids, 2007.

Ukpong, D.P. (a), *Nigerian Pentecostalism: Case, Diagnosis and Prescription,* Fruities Publications, Uyo, 2008.

Ukpong, J.S. (b), "Contextual Hermeneutics: Challenges and Possibilities," J.N.K. Mugambi (eds.) *Text and Context in New Testament Hermeneutics,* Acton Publishers, Nairobi, 2004.

Umoren, Uduakobong E., "Inculturation and the Future of the Church in Africa," Justin S. Ukpong, et al (eds.), *Evangelization in Africa in the Third Millennium: Challenges and Prospects,* CIWA Press, Port Harcourt, 1992.

Usry, Glenn and Craig S. Keener, *Blackman's Religion: Can Christianity Be Afrocentric?* Inter-Varsity Press, Downers Grove, 1996.

Virkler, H.A., *Hermeneutics: Principles and Processes of Bible Interpretation,* Baker Book House, Grand Rapids, 1981.

Wall, A.F., *The Cross Cultural Process in Christian History,* Orbis Books, Maryknoll, 2002.

Wambutda, D.N., "Hebrewisms of West Africa: An Ongoing Search in the Correlations Between the Old Testament and African Weltanschauung," *Obgomosho Journal of Theology*, Number 2, Dec. 1987.

Warrington, K., *Pentecostal Theology: A Theology of Encounter*, T and T Clark, London, 2008.

Wasike, Anne Wasimiyu, "Is Mutuality Possible? An African Response," *Missiology, An International Review*, Vol. XXIX, No. 1, January 2001.

Wilson, N.G., *The Constitution of the Kingdom: A Study on the Sermon on the Mount*, The Westminster Press, 1989.

Witherington III, B. *The Acts of the Apostles: A Socio-Rhetorical Commentary*, Eerdmans, Grand Rapids, 1998.

__________ *The Paul Quest: The Renewed Search for the Jew of Tarsus*, Inter-Varsity Press, Downers Grove, 1998.

Wright, N.T., *What Saint Paul Really Said: Was Paul of Tarsus the Real Founder of Christianity?* Eerdmans Publishing Company, Grand Rapids, 1997.

Young, B.H., *Paul the Jewish Theologian: The Pharisee Among Christians, Jews and Gentiles*, Hendrickson Publishers, Peabody, Massachusetts, 2006.

ACTS PUBLICATIONS

Advanced New Testament Greek	Helleman & Gava
African Christian Theology,	Aben
African Indigenous Churches.	Ayegboyin & Ishola
African Traditional Religion in the Light of the Bible,	Gehman
AIDS is Real and it's in our Church,	Garland & Blyth
Bible Women.	Ekanem
Biblical Preaching in Africa,	Janvier
Biblical Theology of Missions,	Fuller
Celebrating Life,	McCain
Christian Ethics,	Shields
Christianity and Islam,	Abashiya & Ulea
Christianity in Northern Nigeria,	Crampton (update by Gaiya)
Christians in Politics,	Danladi Musa
Churches in Fellowship: The Story of TEKAN,	Hopkins & Gaiya
Cross-cultural Christianity,	Hassan, et al.
Culture and the Christian Home (2nd Ed),	Kore
Discipleship: a West African Perspective,	Janvier & Thaba
Essentials of Christian Religious Studies in Colleges of Ed,	Wiebe, et al, (3 vols.)
Every Abortion Stops a Beating Heart,	Garland & Idoko
Exposition of First Corinthians for Today,	Yamsat

Textbooks for Theological Education in Africa: An Annotated Bibliography,   Starcher & Anguandia

Times of Refreshing: History of Revival in Africa,   Burgess

The Battle is God's   Ferdinando

The Bible and Islam.   Madany

The Work of the Missionary.   Fuller

Theology of the New Testament   Palmer

Theology of the Old Testament,   Palmer

Theology of Worship,   Bartlett

Tough Tests for Top Leaders,   McCain

Train to Teach Others,   Kure

Training for Church Planters.   Janvier

True Minister of God,   Onukwa

Truths for Healthy Churches,   Kore

Turn the Other Cheek,   Kadala

Two Models of Leadership,   McCain

Understanding & Applying the Scriptures,   McCain & Keener

Understanding the Bible,   Stott

Understanding Leadership,   Janvier/Thaba

What A Mess.   Timbuak

We Believe: Introduction on Christian Doctrine,   McCain (2 vols.)

You Could Be a Missionary,   Adekoya

ACTS / HippoBooks / Zondervan titles

African Christian Ethics	Kunhiyop
African Christian Theology	Kunhiyop
God, Where Are You?	Kisoni
Guide to Interpreting Scripture	Kyomya
My Neighbour's Faith (Islam Explained)	Azumah
Preachers of a Different Gospel	Adeleye
The Trinity of Sin	Turaki
The War Within	Chukwuocha

Africa Bible Commentary Series

(ACTS / HippoBooks / Zondervan)

1 & 2 Timothy and Titus	Ngewa
Galatians	Ngewa
Jeremiah and Lamentations	Bungishabaku
Romans	Andria

www.ingramcontent.com/pod-product-compliance
Lightning Source LLC
Chambersburg PA
CBHW051826150726
47998CB00001B/308